EARLY YEARS ACTIVITY CHEST

10-minute games

WITHDRAWN

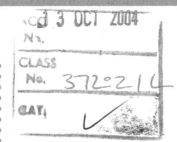

British Library Cataloguing-in-Publication Data
A catalogue record for this book is available from the British Library.

ISBN 0 439 01731 9

ACKNOWLEDGEMENTS

The publishers gratefully acknowledge permission to reproduce the following copyright material:

Irene Yates for 'The parrot parade' © 2000, Irene Yates, previously unpublished.

Every effort has been made to trace copyright holders and the publishers apologize for any inadvertent omissions.

AUTHOR
Barbara J Leach

EDITOR
Clare Miller

ASSISTANT EDITOR
Lesley Sudlow

SERIES DESIGNER
Lynne Joesbury

DESIGNER
Mark Udall

ILLUSTRATIONS
Pete Smith

COVER PHOTOGRAPH
Fiona Pragoff

Text © 2000 Barbara J Leach
© 2000 Scholastic Ltd

Designed using Adobe Pagemaker
Published by Scholastic Ltd, Villiers House,
Clarendon Avenue, Leamington Spa, Warwickshire CV32 5PR

Visit our website at www.scholastic.co.uk

6 7 8 9   4 5 6 7 8

CONTENTS

CONTENTS

Introduction

This book forms part of a series which provides ideas for practical activities across all of the six areas of learning encompassed in the Early Learning Goals for pre-school children. It contains 60 ideas for games and activities lasting up to around ten minutes, that can be used by anyone working in an under-fives setting.

Even with the most meticulous planning, there are inevitably times when, through no fault of your own, you find yourself with an unexpected period of time to fill between one activity and the next. Perhaps the children have tidied away quicker than anticipated or a visitor is late in arriving. Whatever the cause, the outcome remains the same – you have a gap to fill. The games and activities within these pages will help you to use that interlude in a productive and worthwhile way, thus providing a useful alternative to an impromptu song or story session.

Each game requires the minimum of preparation and resources and is designed to allow users to dip in and select activities as required with which to fill those awkward empty moments. Those games which do require some preparation, such as 'Alphabet bingo' on page 20, can often be prepared in advance and kept in a resources pack for use as and when the need arises, thus making them instantly accessible.

You may find it useful to keep the games relating to each area of learning separately in order to find them easily and with the minimum of fuss. The games are adaptable enough to allow users to extend or reduce their length without harming their basic structure, thus making them useful to fill spaces from as little as five minutes, to as long as fifteen. Some games, such as 'Let's make a butterfly' on page 40 and 'Fun with colours' on page 65, require the use of a dice and therefore may last longer than the allotted ten minutes. However, there is no reason why they should not be left part way through and returned to when time allows. The majority of the games are suitable to be played with a large group of up to 20 children, though there are those that are better suited for use with a smaller group of up to only six or ten children.

How to use this book

There are six chapters each comprising ten games or activities and each covering a different area of learning. This allows early years practitioners to easily select games relevant to the area of learning that they wish to focus on at that particular time. There are chapters covering Personal, social and emotional development; Communication, language and literacy; Mathematical development; Knowledge and understanding of the world; Physical development and Creative development. Each activity within these chapters has a clearly defined learning objective closely linked to the Early Learning Goals set out by the Qualifications and Curriculum Authority (QCA).

Although the games contained within this book are primarily designed to be time-fillers, they can also be adapted or extended to become activities for general use to reinforce and consolidate the learning that is already taking place across the whole curriculum. Some of the games, such as 'Spot the mistake' on page 23 and 'How many does that make?' on page 33, have been designed to help the children to develop the skill of rapid thinking. By playing these games regularly, and gradually injecting pace into them, children can be introduced to the kind of rapid thinking that will be required later, when they embark upon the Literacy and Numeracy Hours at statutory school age.

Photocopiable pages

Each chapter is supported by two photocopiable activity sheets that can be used in a variety of ways. Some photocopiable sheets, such as those used in 'Alphabet bingo' on page 20 and 'What shall I wear?' on page 43, are designed as resources to be used for one specific game. Others such as 'Where is it?' used on page 35 can be laminated to make them durable enough to add to the resources already available in your setting. There are also photocopiable sheets such as 'Ceiling, floor, window, door' used on page 49 and 'I sent a postcard to my friend' used on page 51, that are designed to be sent home for the children to use with their parents and carers. These support the home links that are such an important feature in the development of good practice within pre-fives settings. At the same time, these sheets may help to develop a positive attitude within the home towards homework, and may help the children to develop the good habits that will stand them in good stead throughout their school careers.

Using resources

Young children learn through observation, imitation and repetition. Tackling the same activity from a different perspective or through a different medium provides necessary repetition while stimulating the child to take the activity further and so deepen their understanding. It is with this in mind that the activities and games in this book have been designed to utilize a wide variety of resources readily found in most preschool settings, from books and balloons to musical instruments and old teddies. However, some games may require nothing more than the presence of a thoughtful adult and a group of lively children! 'Forfeit fish' on page 22, utilizes the magnets that young children always find so fascinating, while 'Pass it along' on page 32, involves the use of flat, geometric shapes. Some activities, such as 'And then...' on page 24, provide the practitioner with the opportunity to involve the children in the selection of their own resources, giving even the most reticent child a sense of involvement right from the start.

Links with home

There is a small section at the end of each activity that gives suggestions on ways to keep parents and carers actively involved in their children's learning. 'Home links' provides various ideas for keeping parents and carers informed about what their children have been doing during their day, as well as helping them to continue their child's learning at home and through this, keep in touch with their progress.

Sometimes, as in 'Alphabet bingo' on page 20, there may be a completed sheet to send home to encourage parents and carers to work on a specific task with their child. Other times, there might be a suggestion for a more open-ended activity, such as 'I guess...' on page 36. Often there will be a suggestion for a practical activity to be completed at home

and brought back to be shared with the rest of the group, thus making the links a two-way thing.

Finally, there will be the occasional photocopiable sheet, such as that used in 'Ceiling, floor, window, door' on page 49, that is designed to be completed at home as a follow-up to the group game in order to consolidate the learning that has taken place.

Multicultural links

Several activities suggest ideas for ways to ensure that the cultural diversity of our society is reflected in our work with children. In doing this, we can help children to understand and value the wide range of faiths and beliefs that are to be found in our world. The suggestions also provide a starting point for forging further valuable links with home and the local community.

Winning and losing

There are many arguments both for and against the need for competitiveness among children, but most people would agree that it is not particularly pleasant to be a loser! The games in this book are therefore primarily concerned with having fun while learning, and the vast majority of them are non-competitive. There are, however, the odd one or two, such as 'Listen and move' on page 57, that can be played as elimination games if desired. There are also some team games, such as 'Pass it on' on page 55, that encourage competitiveness between teams of players, but as the make-up of the teams is likely to be different every time you play, there should be no build-up of unhealthy rivalry among members. The vast majority of the activities in this book encourage competition not against opponents but against yourself, the clock or perhaps an inanimate object such as the ball in 'Dribble and trap' on page 58.

Finally, it is hoped that the games that are contained in this book will provide short fun-filled activities for young children and those working with them. It is also anticipated that they will inspire both providers and children to invent their own games and activities to fill any idle moments, and to share these with their friends and families both within the group and at home.

Personal, social and emotional development

The games in this chapter encourage children to interact with their peers with increasing confidence and understanding. Through these activities children are given the opportunity to work as a team, to express and share ideas, and to think about helping and caring for others.

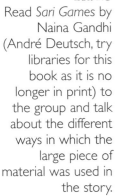

WHO'S MISSING?

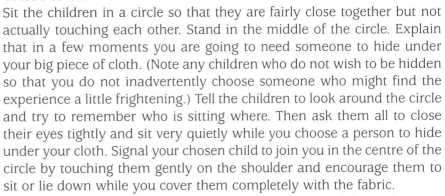

Learning objectives
To concentrate and sit quietly when appropriate; to be confident to try a new activity and share ideas with a group.

What you need
A large piece of dark but lightweight material.

Preparation
Ensure that the children are familiar with each other's names.

What to do
Sit the children in a circle so that they are fairly close together but not actually touching each other. Stand in the middle of the circle. Explain that in a few moments you are going to need someone to hide under your big piece of cloth. (Note any children who do not wish to be hidden so that you do not inadvertently choose someone who might find the experience a little frightening.) Tell the children to look around the circle and try to remember who is sitting where. Then ask them all to close their eyes tightly and sit very quietly while you choose a person to hide under your cloth. Signal your chosen child to join you in the centre of the circle by touching them gently on the shoulder and encourage them to sit or lie down while you cover them completely with the fabric.

Invite the children to open their eyes and look around the circle to see who is missing. If no immediate answer is forthcoming, begin giving clues. Ask the hidden child to say whether they are a boy or a girl, uncover the child's hand or foot, or point to the empty space in the circle to show them where the child was sitting before being hidden. Continue giving clues and revealing more and more of the child until their identity has been guessed. Repeat the process with a different child.

Support
Use a screen at the front of the group to hide the children if they are in any way unhappy with the idea of being covered by the fabric.

Extension
Encourage the children to ask questions to help them discover the identity of the hidden child.

FARMYARD FRIENDS

Learning objectives

To take part confidently in a large and noisy group activity; to understand the need for agreed codes of behaviour.

What you need

The photocopiable sheet on page 70; a large open space where noise will not cause a nuisance to others.

Preparation

Copy the photocopiable sheet four times onto thin card and cut along the lines to make sixteen individual animal cards.

What to do

Gather the children together and look at each animal card in turn. Practise making the sounds of the different animals in soft voices. Explain to the children that you are going to play a game where everyone is making a noise at the same time, so they must try not to use loud voices or everyone will get a headache! Ask the group to spread out and find a space where they can sit or stand by themselves. Shuffle the animal cards and give one card to each child.

Explain that when the children are given the signal, they must begin to make the sound of the animal shown on their card and move around the area trying to find other children making the same sound so that they can join together in a group. When all the children are sorted into their animal groups, finish the game by singing 'Old MacDonald Had a Farm', using those groups.

Support

Some very young children may need help to cope with this rather noisy and confusing activity, so be ready to encourage and assist them throughout the game.

Extension

Use word cards rather than picture cards and encourage the children to move like the animal whose sound they are making.

GROUP SIZE
Whole group.

HOLD TIGHT!

Learning objective

To work together as a team.

What you need

A large piece of colourful, lightweight fabric; a small sponge ball; a large open space.

What to do

Spread out the fabric on the floor and ask each child to find a place to sit around its perimeter. Explain that they should sit slightly away from the material so that their feet do not touch it. Then ask each child to grasp the edge of the fabric in an overhand grip and lift it just a few centimetres off the floor. Place the ball in the centre of the fabric and let the group experiment by gently lifting and lowering the edge of the material to make the ball roll this way and that without falling off the edge. Remind the children to grasp the fabric firmly all the time and to stay seated around its edge.

Once the children are familiar with this activity, explain that you are going to call a child's name and that they must all work together to try to get the ball to roll to that child. That child then calls another child's name and the ball is directed to her. The game finishes when the ball has been sent to every child.

Support

Have an adult between every three or four children to help guide the lowering and lifting of the fabric.

Extension

Let older children stand rather than sit for this game and encourage them to invent similar games to be played with the material. Try using two balls and directing each one to a different child at the same time, or cut a hole in the fabric and use it either as an obstacle to be avoided or as a goal to aim for.

HOME LINKS
Borrow or hire a full-size playchute and invite parents and carers in to play a variety of games with the children. (A booklet of games is usually provided with each playchute.)

MULTICULTURAL LINKS
Sari material is an ideal fabric for this activity as it is lightweight and can be obtained in a variety of vibrant colours.

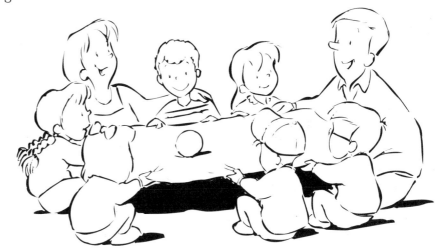

LET'S GET TOGETHER

Learning objective
To mix confidently and harmoniously with adults and peers.

What you need
A large defined area, either indoors or out.

Preparation
Gather the children together and ensure that everyone understands where the boundaries of the playing area are. Practise running around within that area without bumping into one another and on a given signal – clapped hands or verbal 'stop!' – standing very still and listening carefully.

What to do
Tell the children that once they have stopped very still you are going to call out a number and they must get into groups of that size. Practise once or twice with numbers two and three, checking the groups each time by counting and helping the children to solve any little problems that occur with prompts such as, 'Hmm! We seem to have three in this group instead of two. How can we put that right?'. (The adult could join hands with the extra child to make another group.) If there are any children who cannot find a group, suggest that they come to you to see if there are any other spare children that they can join with. Then play the game using random numbers up to five. Each time a new group is formed, encourage its members to introduce themselves to each other such as, 'Hello, I'm Krishna' before continuing the game.

Finish the game by calling out the total number of children in the group so that they all join in a circle together. Ask one child to count around the circle to check that there are the correct number of children. Congratulate the children on their excellent counting and grouping and suggest that they might like to play again another day, perhaps using bigger numbers to make it more difficult.

Support
Use only the number two throughout the game, so that the children are continually finding new partners to introduce themselves to.

Extension
Use larger numbers and instead of calling them out, hold up the written digit for the children to see and recognize.

GROUP SIZE
Whole group.

HOP SWAP

Learning objective
To actively take part in a large group activity.

What you need
A light, comfortable blindfold; a large space.

What to do
Gather the group together in a circle. Explain that you are going to call out the names of two children and that they must swap places with each other by hopping across the circle. Practise this a few times with different pairs of children. Then ask a child to wear a blindfold and stand in the centre of the circle. Tie the blindfold loosely and ask her to spread out her arms and listen carefully so that she knows which way to move, because this time when you call out the children's names she must try to touch them as they change places across the circle. If a child is touched, then he takes his place in the centre of the circle and the game continues. If a child is not caught after three 'hop swaps', ask another child to wear the blindfold. The game continues until everybody has had a turn to hop across the circle at least once.

Support
Be aware that some children may not want to wear a blindfold. If such a child is caught and does not wish to play in the centre, ask him to choose another child instead.

Extension
Rather than hopping, encourage the swappers to slither on their tummies or shuffle on their bottoms to reach the other side of the circle. Alternatively, increase the level of difficulty for them by having two blindfolded players at a time in the centre of the circle.

HOME LINKS
Ask parents and carers to tell you about blindfold games from their own childhood and consider gathering them into a book to add to the group's resource bank.

GROUP SIZE
Up to ten children.

REMEMBER, REMEMBER

Learning objective
To take turns to recall items removed from a collection.

What you need
A collection of approximately 12 different objects of any kind; a bag to put them in.

Preparation
Before beginning the game ensure that the children are all familiar with and can name all the objects in your collection.

What to do
Gather the children into a circle and place the objects in the centre in full view of everyone. Hold up the items one by one, asking the children to say each name aloud. Repeat the process, this time placing each object inside the bag as it is named. Once all the objects are in the bag, ask the children to close their eyes and think hard for a few seconds about what is in the bag. Then ask each child in turn around the circle to name just one of the objects in the bag. As each correct item is named, take it out of the bag and replace it in the centre of the circle. If an incorrect item is named, look in the bag and say, 'Sorry, I don't have a (torch) in my bag, but I do have a...'. (Give a clue to one of the remaining items and invite the child to guess what it might be.) The game continues until all the items have been named and the bag is empty.

Support
Invite very young children to select an object one by one, say what it is and put it into the bag. When it is their turn to recall an item, it may help if they then think about what they or a friend put into the bag.

Extension
Put 20 items into the collection and include some which the children may not be quite so familiar with. Scoop all the objects into the bag at once rather than one by one.

HOME LINKS

Encourage parents and carers to improve their children's memories by playing 'Do you remember...?' and asking their child to recall details about recent events such as last week's trip to the swimming pool or yesterday's dinner.

MULTICULTURAL LINKS

Include in your collection items from various countries and cultures such as castanets, clogs, a boomerang or chopsticks, and talk about them before you begin the game.

SECRET SHOPPING

Learning objective
To select resources independently.

What you need
The photocopiable sheet on page 71; two sets of the ten objects shown on the photocopiable sheet; pen; two small tables; two boxes; a screen; two bags.

Preparation
Make two copies of the photocopiable sheet and circle six different objects on each one. Put a set of ten objects on each of the two tables and place one on either side of the screen. Invite a team of children to sit in front of each table. Sit several feet away, facing the children, with an empty box either side of you.

What to do
Explain to the children that you are going to play 'Secret shopping' and that they will need to be very quiet and to listen carefully. Tell the children that you are going to whisper a message to someone and that they will whisper to someone else who will go shopping. Choose a child to have a trial run to demonstrate. Call the child to you and whisper his message, 'Tell Jani to bring me a book'. Then give him a bag and send him off to deliver his message and give Jani the bag.

Jani then goes to her team's table, selects the item, puts it in the bag and carries it back to you to put in your box. Then give Jani a message to deliver to the next member of her team. Have a few practices to ensure that everyone knows what to do before beginning the game properly. Use the photocopiable sheets as shopping lists and continue the game until each child has had a turn to both carry the message and to shop, and six items have been collected in each box. Finish the game by checking the items in the boxes against the appropriate shopping list to see how many are correct. Congratulate the teams on any successes.

Support
Ask very young or less able children to repeat the message back to you to ensure they have heard and understood it correctly.

Extension
Complicate your messages by adding extra detail such as, 'Please ask Jani to kindly fetch me the small book that she will find in the middle of the table'.

GROUP SIZE
Whole group.

HOW DO YOU DO?

Learning objectives
To be confident to speak in a familiar group; to work together harmoniously.

What you need
The traditional finger rhyme 'Tommy Thumb, Tommy Thumb' (*This Little Puffin...*, compiled by Elizabeth Matterson, Puffin).

Preparation
Ensure that the children are familiar with the rhyme 'Tommy Thumb, Tommy Thumb'.

What to do
Say or sing the rhyme through with the children, doing the accompanying actions. Explain that you are going to say (or sing) it through again but that this time you are not going to use fingers, you are going to use the children. Choose two children to start the game and sit one on either side of you. Say the rhyme through, substituting finger names with children's names: 'Nini and Jas, Nini and Jas; Where are you? Where are you?'. Prompt the two named children to stand up in turn to say, 'Here I am', 'Here I am', and to shake hands with one another as they say, 'How do you do?'. Remind the group to listen very carefully so that when they hear their name they can stand up and say 'Here I am'.

Continue the game using a different pair of children for each verse until everyone has had at least one turn to shake hands with someone else. Finish with the last verse of the rhyme, 'Children all, Children all; Where are you? Where are you?'. Signal all of the children to stand up and say together, 'Here we are, Here we are' and to shake hands with each other as they say their final, 'How do you do?'.

Support
If some of the children are reluctant to stand and speak aloud in a large group situation, make sure that you pair them with yourself so that they can speak along with you and remain seated if they prefer.

Extension
Use surnames rather than first names with slightly older children – 'Miss Rahm and Master Sidat, Miss Rahm and Master Sidat; Where are you? Where are you?'.

HOME LINKS
Ask parents and carers to help their children to compile a list of the many different ways that they greet people over the course of the next few days, for example, Hello; How are you?; Hi; and bring it in to share with the rest of the group.

MULTICULTURAL LINKS
Try using another language such as French for the responses, 'Je suis ici'; and 'Bonjour mon ami'.

GROUP SIZE
Whole group.

A GAME CALLED 'IF'

Learning objective
To be aware of and sensitive to the views of others.

What you need
Yourself and the children!

What to do
Gather the children into a circle and tell them that you are going to play a thinking game called 'If'. Explain that it is a very easy game because you can think of all sorts of things that you would really like to do, as long as you remember to begin with the word, 'If'. The first time you play this game it is a good idea to let an adult start, but once the children are familiar with it they will be able to start subsequent games themselves.

Begin the game with a fanciful idea such as, 'If I could fly, I would go to the moon and build myself a big palace and put a big bouncy castle right in the middle and I'd bounce and bounce and bounce really, really high. What would you do...?'. Look around the circle and choose a child to either continue with your idea or come up with one of her own. Continue the game until everyone who wants to has had a turn and finish by briefly recalling some of the ideas and marvelling at the children's inventiveness.

Support
Encourage reluctant speakers with questions and prompts to get their ideas flowing.

Extension
Change the game to 'What if?' for older children and encourage them to put forward thought-provoking questions and to think of inventive solutions to them such as, 'What if we had no paper?', 'What if the sea suddenly dried up?', 'What if the sun stopped shining?'.

HOME LINKS
Encourage parents and carers to write an 'If' book for their children to illustrate and bring in to share with the group.

MULTICULTURAL LINKS
Encourage discussion about other countries and cultures by starting an 'If' game with, 'If I lived in India.'.. and have a range of informative books nearby for reference.

GROUP SIZE
Whole group.

CAN I HELP YOU?

Learning objective
To develop an awareness of the needs and feelings of others.

What you need
A selection of photographs or pictures showing people in situations where help might be required such as a crying baby, a child in a wheelchair, someone with a broken limb, a person who has dropped their shopping or spilled something, a child who has fallen over.

What to do
Put the pictures face down on a surface and ask a child to choose one to share with the group. Look at the picture together and discuss it. Ask the children to try to imagine what they would feel like if they were the person in the picture. Why might the baby be crying? (hunger, thirst, tiredness, fear, pain, discomfort). How might she be comforted? (gentle rocking, cuddling, feeding, singing).

When all your ideas have been exhausted, invite another child to select a second picture and repeat the process of discussing the subject's feelings and then thinking of ways to help or comfort them. After seven or eight minutes, draw the game to a close by briefly recalling the pictures used and recapping on the helpful ideas that were suggested. Ask the children to try to remember those ideas so that they might be able to use them one day to help a friend in distress.

Support
Be aware that some young children may become upset if a picture reminds them of a distressing event in their past, so be ready to offer lots of support and comfort.

Extension
Ask two children to decide together which picture to choose and to act out the situation shown, with one taking the part of the subject and the other taking the part of the comforter.

HOME LINKS
Suggest that parents and carers keep a 'Help book' with their children for a week, recording at least one helpful thing that the children do each day. These could include setting the table, making their bed, tidying away toys without being told or reading a book to a younger brother or sister.

MULTICULTURAL LINKS
Display books and pictures showing children from all over the world helping others. Include situations more normally found in the developing world – children carrying infants strapped to their backs, washing clothes in rivers, carrying water to their houses – as well as more familiar activities such as helping with the shopping, cuddling a distressed friend and helping to do up shoes or coats.

This chapter provides a range of ideas for consolidating learning through short, easily digested activities. Ideas include helping children to practise careful listening, identifying letters and their sound, and recognizing familiar words.

Communication, language and literacy

GROUP SIZE
Up to ten children.

THE PARROT PARADE

Learning objective
To sustain attentive listening, responding to what has been heard by relevant actions.

What you need
The photocopiable sheet on page 69; a small piece of coloured card for each child (same colours as in the story).

What to do
Gather the children together and explain that you are going to read them a story and that they must listen very carefully for any colours that are mentioned in it. Give each child a piece of coloured card, ensuring that each one recognizes the colour that they have been given. Now tell the children that when they hear their own particular colour mentioned in the story they must stand up, turn around and sit down again. Call out a few phrases as a practice to make sure that everyone knows what to do, then read the story. At first you may need to read more slowly than normal and perhaps even emphasize the colour words, but once you have played the game a few times the children will become familiar with it and their responses will become much quicker.

Support
Have some pieces of coloured card close at hand while reading the story and hold up the relevant colour as you read its name so that the younger or less able children can match their colour to yours.

Extension
Secondary colours are included in the story but give out only primary colour cards so that children have to stand up in pairs to make the relevant colour – red and yellow to make orange, blue and red to make purple, and so on.

HOME LINKS

Encourage parents and carers to play colour I-spy with their children to help them to recognize a wide range of colours.

MULTICULTURAL LINKS

Adapt and use an appropriate multicultural story such as *Max* by Ken Wilson (David Bennett Books) or *Kofi and the Butterflies* by Sandra Horn (Tamarind).

GROUP SIZE
Up to eight children.

ALPHABET BINGO

Learning objective
To link sounds to the letters of the alphabet.

What you need
The photocopiable sheet on page 72; pencil for each child; pencil and paper for the adult.

Preparation
For each game you intend to play, make two copies of the photocopiable sheet and cut along the lines to make eight bingo sheets.

What to do
Explain that you are going to play a game of bingo and show one of the sheets to the group. Tell them that you are going to call out a letter sound and that they must look for the matching letter on their sheet. If they find it, they must put a ring around it with their pencil. When all the letters on their sheet have a ring around them they must put up their hand and call 'alphabet'. Give each child a bingo sheet and a pencil and ask them to write their name on the back of it.

When everyone is ready, begin to call out the letter sounds and make a note of each one as you call it. (The letters x and z are not included on the sheets.) When a child calls 'alphabet', use your list to check his card. (If eight children are playing there should, of course, be two winners.) The winners can then become the caller and the caller's assistant whose job it is to record the letters called.

Support
As you call each letter sound, write the letter shape on a board for the children to see so that they can match it visually as well as aurally.

Extension
Instead of calling the letter sound, call a word that begins with that sound so that the children have to work hard to hear and isolate the initial sound. Keep a record of the word that you called rather than just the sound, to help the children to understand any mistakes that they may have made.

HOME LINKS
Send home the used bingo sheets and ask parents to help their children to learn those particular letters and their sounds, perhaps by playing I spy, Hunt the object or Alphabet bingo.

GROUP SIZE
Up to ten children.

INITIALS

Learning objective
To hear and use initial sounds.

What you need
A pencil and paper and a flat surface for every child; a whiteboard and marker pen.

What to do
Tell the children that you are going to see how many things they can think of that begin with the same letter. Explain that they will have only five minutes to draw or write as many as they can and then you will count them up to see how many different ones they have managed to think of. Explain also that the drawings do not have to be beautifully detailed as they are just to remind them of the objects that they thought of.

When this game is first played, give the children an easy letter such as 's', and if they still seem to be struggling, give continual clues by touching or standing near appropriate items – sink, scissors, sock, scarf – as you say the sound.

After the allotted five minutes, ask the children to put down their pencils and begin to tell you the items that they have on their paper. List the items on the whiteboard as they are called out and keep a record of the total for future reference. Compare the results with those from any subsequent games and remark upon any improvements that have been made.

Vary the instructions sometimes to keep the game interesting, asking the children to think of only animals that begin with a particular letter or only things taller than themselves.

Support
Ask the children to find and collect actual objects in the room rather than writing them down or drawing them.

Extension
Use blends such as 'sh' or 'str' instead of single letter sounds.

HOME LINKS
Ask parents and carers to play I spy with their children while out shopping or working around the house.

GROUP SIZE
Up to ten children.

FORFEIT FISH

Learning objective
To recognize and read familiar names and words.

What you need
One small cardboard fish for each child plus a few extras; felt-tipped pen; paper clips; a small magnet tied to a piece of string; a bowl or basin.

Preparation
Write a child's name on one side of each fish and a number on each of the extra ones. Fix a paper clip to the nose of each fish. Make some 'forfeit cards' by writing a number on one side of a small piece of card and instructions on the other, such as hop on one leg, sing a song, count up to ten, build a tower, and so on.

What to do
Gather the children together and show them the fish. Let them practise recognizing and reading the names. Look at the spare fish. What do they have on the back of them? Explain that the numbers will tell them to do something. Look at each one in turn and read out the words together. Show the children the fishing-rod and demonstrate how the magnet attracts the paper clip to catch a fish. Then place all the fish, written side down, in the bowl and choose an 'angler' to start the game. When the child catches a fish she reads out the name on the back and that child becomes the new angler. If a number card is caught, the child has to complete the forfeit before trying to catch another fish.

Support
When a child catches a fish, encourage him to hold it up for the whole group to see and to read together.

Extension
Include more forfeit fish and encourage the angler to read the forfeit card himself.

HOME LINKS
Ask parents and carers to encourage their children to learn to recognize and write their own name and the names of members of their family.

GROUP SIZE
Whole group.

SPOT THE MISTAKE

Learning objective
To sustain attentive listening, responding to what they have heard by relevant comments.

What you need
A favourite story; a whiteboard and marker pen.

HOME LINKS
Explain to the children that sometimes when people are talking quickly they make mistakes. Ask them to listen very carefully at home and see if they can spot any mistakes being made. (Warn parents and carers that you have asked the children to do this as they might not take kindly to their children correcting them!)

MULTICULTURAL LINKS
Remember to regularly use stories from other cultures as well as traditional English fairy-tales for this exercise, and be aware that children to whom English is a second language may have difficulties with pronunciation or grammatical differences, so keep your errors contextual.

What to do
Gather the children together and explain that you are going to read them a story that they know well and have enjoyed before. Tell them that this time when you read it you are going to make some mistakes and that they should listen very carefully and stop you as soon as they hear a mistake. The children should then tell you what you have said wrong and what the correct word should have been. Write your name on one half of the board and 'children' on the other. Explain that every time they spot a mistake you will make a mark on their half of the board, and every time they fail to spot one you will put a mark on your half and tell them what they missed. Begin to read the story, making mistakes as you go and tallying the score on the board. At the end of the story count up all the marks to see who has won.

Support
Read the story at a slower pace than normal and make the mistakes glaringly obvious at first, gradually speeding up as the children get used to the game.

Extension
Read at normal speed and make the mistakes subtle, for example use 'she' instead of 'he' or replace a word with another that sounds very similar but does not make sense, such as 'I'll huff and I'll puff and I'll bow your house down'.

AND THEN...

Learning objectives

To use talk to organize and sequence events; to interact with others, negotiating plans and taking turns in conversation.

What you need

A bag containing an assortment of everyday items such as a shoe, an old teddy, a letter. (Once the children have become familiar with this activity they might like to select items of their own for inclusion in the bag.)

What to do

Sit the children in a circle and explain that you had a story in your bag but you dropped the bag and the story got broken! Now you can't remember what the story was and it's all muddled up. Ask the children if they could help you to put the pieces back together again to make a story that's as good as new.

Empty all of the things out of the bag into the centre of the circle and ask the children what they think the story might have started with. If no suggestions are forthcoming, then choose an item yourself from the pile and begin a tale: 'I think perhaps the story started with... a shoe (take the shoe from the heap). This shoe belonged to a very grumpy man who lived in a tiny house, far away from everyone'. Think aloud so as to involve the children in the story: 'I wonder why he lived so far from everyone? And I wonder why this shoe was so important?'. As the children become involved, encourage them to select items from the centre and explain their part in the story. Be ready to help by weaving their various ideas together to make a coherent and satisfying story.

Support

Fill your bag with items from a familiar story such as 'The Three Little Pigs' or 'Little Red Riding Hood' and help the children to select the items in sequence and to retell the story in their own words.

Extension

Look at all the items together and then replace them in the bag. Ask a child to start the story using whichever item he chooses before passing the bag to the next person in the circle, who then selects a different item and continues the story to include that item before passing the bag on to the next person. The story ends when the bag is empty.

WHO DO YOU THINK IT IS?

Learning objectives
To recognize their own names; to link letters to familiar words.

What you need
A large whiteboard and marker pen; name cards for all of the children present.

Preparation
Gather the group around the board and go through the name cards carefully to ensure that each child recognizes at least his own name. Count the number of letters in each name before placing the cards near the board so that they can be clearly seen by all of the children.

What to do
Tell the children you are going to see if they can work out whose name you are thinking of by guessing its letters. Choose a child's name from those present and put a horizontal line on the board for each letter it contains (as in 'Hangman').

Explain that the children have to guess a letter for you to write in the name but that if it doesn't belong then you will begin to draw a face. Tell them that they must try to guess the whole name before the face is completed. Invite the children to take turns to choose a letter for you to write on the line, if appropriate. Each time that they choose a letter that is not in the name, keep a record of it at the bottom of the board and draw a part of a face. (Start with the outline and leave the mouth until last so that if the children are successful and guess the name correctly you can add a smiling face and if they fail you can add a sad one.)

Support
Begin the game by writing in the initial letter of the name that you have chosen.

Extension
Remove the name cards for older or more able children and sometimes include the name of a child not actually present in the group at the time.

GROUP SIZE
Up to eight
children.

WHAT'S THE LETTER?

Learning objective
To identify individual letters by touch only and read them independently.

What you need
An alphabet cut from sandpaper (a wooden alphabet could be used instead); a large cardboard box, Blu-Tack or similar; scissors; an alphabet chart large enough for all of the children to see.

Preparation
Cut a hole just large enough for a child to insert his hand and arm in one side of the upturned box. Attach a sandpaper letter with Blu-Tack to the table-top and place the box over it so that it cannot be seen. Place the alphabet chart in clear view near the box.

What to do
Gather the children in front of the table and show them some of the letters. Pass them around and let them feel the roughness of the sandpaper. Invite them to close their eyes and trace their fingers over the letters to feel their shape. Then collect up all the letters and tell the children that you have put one of the letters under the box. Explain that you have stuck it to the table so that they can feel its sandpaper shape and try to guess what it is.

Invite a child to be first to put her hand in the box. As she feels the letter, remind her to think hard about its shape. Is it curved or straight? Is it tall or short? Encourage her to look at the alphabet chart and find the letter that she thinks is like the one under the box. Lift the box to see if she is correct. If she isn't, give her the sandpaper letter and help her to match it to the one on the chart, reinforcing her correct choice by talking about the shape of the letter as well as its name and sound: 'That's right. It's a 'k' isn't it? It's a tall letter that's made of straight lines. Well done!'.

Support
Use a limited number of letters to play the game, concentrating at first on those with distinctive shapes such as 'o', 's', 'k' and 'l'.

Extension
Remove the alphabet chart from the view of older or more able children and encourage them to give both the letter's name and its sound.

HOME LINKS
Explain to parents
and carers that you
have been guessing
letters by feeling
their shape and
encourage them to
play 'feel-and-guess'
games at home with
their children using
various household
objects or toys.

GROUP SIZE
Up to 12 children.

WHAT NONSENSE!

Learning objectives

To experiment with sounds and words; to listen attentively, responding to what is heard with relevant actions.

What you need

A selection of books with strong rhymes and a touch of nonsense humour, such as *The Cat in the Hat* by Dr Seuss (Collins).

Preparation

Gather the group together and enjoy sharing one of the books. Read it through a few times, the last time letting the children add the rhyming words at the end of each line. Talk about rhymes being words that sound the same and spend some time thinking of words that rhyme with familiar everyday objects.

What to do

Tell the children that you are going to talk to them using some wrong words and that they must try to guess what the right words are. Explain that you will use a rhyming word in place of the real word and have a short practice using very obvious substitutions such as, 'Jack and Jill went up the pill'. Then begin to use ordinary sentences in which to make your substitutions such as, 'I am tired so I think I will go to Ned'.

As the children become adept at this game, you can begin to make multiple substitutions to really get them listening and thinking hard: 'I was walking gnome last tight when I saw a dig crown log humming towards me'. At first, you may need to speak at a slower pace than normal but eventually you will be able to talk at normal speed. To keep track of how well your substitutions are being spotted, tell the children to listen very carefully and every time they hear you say a wrong word, they must shoot their hand up into the air and then put it down again.

Support

Use nursery rhymes or familiar stories for your substitutions in order to give contextual clues to support those with less well-developed listening skills: 'Once upon a time there were three cares – Mummy Care, Daddy Care and Little Baby Care'.

Extension

Ask older or more able children to count in their heads the number of substitutions that they hear you make in each sentence and to try to recall them all only after you have finished speaking.

HOME LINKS

Put a toy cat on a display table and ask parents and carers to help their children bring something from home that rhymes with 'cat'.

MULTICULTURAL LINKS
Share some Caribbean rhymes with the group, such as those in *A Caribbean Counting Book* by Faustin Charles and Roberta Arenson (Barefoot Books), and try inventing some 'rap' songs to practise rhyming.

FIND AND CUT

Learning objective
To identify given letters and talk about their name and sound.

What you need
Old newspapers; scissors; small empty tub or bowl; a whiteboard and marker pen.

Preparation
Unfold the newspapers into separate sheets and check to make sure that their contents are suitable for young children to work with.

What to do
Ensure that the children are seated safely either on the floor or at a table before giving them each a pair of scissors and a sheet of newspaper and placing the small bowl in easy reach of everyone. Explain that you are going to write a letter on the board and that the children must look through their newspaper and try to find as many of that letter as they can, then cut them out and put them in the bowl.

Write your chosen letter on the board and look at it with the children. Talk about its name, shape and sound and ask each child to show you one in his paper. Then give the children five minutes or so to find and cut out their letters.

When the time is up, ask all of the children to put down their scissors and together examine and count the cut-out letters. Talk again about the letter names and sounds and put them to one side for future use in collage work or sorting activities.

Support
Work with only four children at a time and use enlarged photocopies of newspaper sections and highlighter pens instead of scissors to identify the letters.

Extension
Challenge older children to think of a different word for every letter that they have managed to cut out, so the larger their collection the more words they must think of.

CHAPTER 3

Mathematical development

Extend children's understanding of basic mathematical concepts through these fun activities. They include using number cards to understand more and less and to carry out simple arithmetic, and to recognize geometric shapes by touch.

MORE OR LESS

Learning objectives
To recognize numerals 1 to 5; to develop an understanding of 'more' and 'less'.

What you need
Two sets of A4 cards each bearing a different number from 1 to 5.

Preparation
Talk about the cards with the children and practise finding numbers that are more or less than a given number.

What to do
Gather the children together and choose five children to stand in a line with their backs to the group. Show them the cards before shuffling them and giving one to each of the five children. Do not let the main group of children see the numbers. Explain that they are going to take turns to guess whether the next child in line is holding a number that is more or less than the one already shown.

Turn the first child around. Ask the group what number she is holding. Choose a child to guess whether the next number will be more or less than the first one. Turn the second child around. If the guess was correct, the game continues with another child guessing the next card and so on until all five numbers are shown. If the guess was incorrect (including if the next number is the same), the game stops. The child or children who have shown their numbers sit down to join the group and more are selected to take their place at the end of the line. The ongoing group challenge is to get all five cards shown. Keep a record of the most cards turned and try to beat that the next time you play the game.

Alternatively, if you have a very successful session when playing this game, then keep a record of how many times the children completed the challenge. Compare it with the success rate of subsequent games that the children play.

Support
Use three sets of cards bearing only the numbers 1, 2 and 3.

Extension
Use two sets of 11 cards, bearing the numbers 0 to 10, and introduce the word 'equals' for any matching pairs that appear.

I CAN SEE

Learning objective
To develop and extend mathematical vocabulary.

What you need
An area containing plenty of mathematical objects such as regular geometric shapes, numbers and groups of objects in various amounts, plus the normal collection of tables, chairs and toys.

What to do
This game is a mathematical version of the more familiar game of I spy. To start, chant, 'I know what I can see and...'. Give a brief description of the item that you are thinking of, using mathematical language, for example, 'It's got four legs'. Let the children try to guess what it is. Reinforce intelligent guesses with encouraging remarks such as, 'That was a good idea – the table. The table has got four legs but it's not what I'm thinking about at the moment. Can you think of something else that has got four legs and is in this room?' Choose a wide variety of objects and descriptions so that the children become familiar with a range of mathematical terms covering not just number, but also shape, size and position.

As the children become familiar with the game, some may be able to take over the role of choosing and describing the object to be guessed. It is a good idea for the child to whisper to the adult which item he has chosen along with its description so that any necessary adjustments can be made before presenting his ideas to the group.

Support
Work with a group of only four to six children and encourage them to locate the chosen object physically rather than just trying to see it.

Extension
Use mathematically precise language to describe objects, for example, 'I know what I can see and... it has eight corners and six square faces' (a cube or dice).

GROUP SIZE
Whole group.

GUESS WHO!

Learning objective
To recognize simple patterns and to solve practical problems.

What you need
Yourself and the children!

What to do
Tell the children that they must listen carefully and see if they can guess which one of them you are describing. Mentally, choose a child and begin to describe her aloud to the group. Make your first sentence quite generalized so that it could be applied equally well to more than one child in the group such as, 'This child is not a boy'. Ask the group who it might be and agree that it could indeed be any of the girls. Invite the girls to stand at the front of the group as you add the next piece of your description, for example, 'She has her hair in a ponytail'. Again, ask the group which of the girls this applies to and let those who are eliminated sit down again. Continue in this way, describing in more and more detail and eliminating candidates until there is only one possible solution. When there is just one child left, congratulate the group and remind them why that particular child must be the one. 'That's right, Mina is the only girl who has a ponytail, lace-up shoes and three buttons on her cardigan. Well done!'

Vary the game by choosing several children who have something in common with each other but not the rest of the group, such as a particular style of shirt, shoe colour or fabric pattern. Ask them to stand at the front of the group and let the other children guess what they have in common.

Support
Simplify your clues by concentrating on obvious details such as colour of clothing or child's gender.

Extension
Rather than bringing a group of 'possibles' to the front and gradually eliminating them, give a brief but detailed description of your chosen subject right at the start, and let the group work out its own elimination processes until they find the right solution.

HOME LINKS
Ask parents and carers to help their children to identify similarities and differences between everyday objects such as items of clothing or patterns on crockery.

PASS IT ALONG

Learning objectives
To begin to understand the properties of various regular geometric shapes; to use language such as 'circle' or 'big' to describe flat shapes.

What you need
A soft fabric bag; a set of flat geometric shapes such as triangles, squares, circles and rectangles in various sizes and thicknesses.

Preparation
Gather the children together and look at the shapes. Pass them around for the children to touch and talk about. Discuss such things as straight sides and curved edges and notice how the corners of some shapes are more pointed than others. Familiarize the children with the names of the various shapes and notice how many corners each one has.

What to do
Put all the shapes together into the bag and sit the group in a circle in which you are included. Dip your hand into the bag and feel for a shape without looking. Say, 'I think I will find…' (choose a particular shape to find) '…a triangle'. Hold up the shape you have selected and let the group judge whether you were successful or not. If you have selected the correct shape keep it, if you haven't then put it back in the bag. Continue by passing the bag to the child next to you and inviting him to say what shape he intends to find as he dips his hand into the bag (no peeping!). Encourage him to tell the group about the shape he can feel before revealing it: 'I think it's a circle because I can't feel any corners'. Again, if the selected shape is correct it is kept, if incorrect it is returned to the bag. Play continues around the circle until the bag is empty or until every child has had a turn.

Once the children are familiar with this activity, they can be challenged to find shapes which fulfil two or more criteria – a big square; a small, thick rectangle.

Support
Use shapes of only one size and thickness so that very young or less able children can concentrate on shape alone.

Extension
Introduce the idea of negative properties and challenge the children to find a shape that is *not* thick, *not* a circle and *not* large.

HOW MANY DOES THAT MAKE?

Learning objectives

To begin to use the vocabulary involved in adding; to practise simple mental arithmetic.

What you need

The photocopiable sheet on page 73; coloured paper or card; scissors.

Preparation

Make four copies of the top half of the photocopiable sheet, each copy on a different colour, then cut them out to make four sets of numbers 1 to 5. (Laminate them for a lasting finish.)

What to do

Gather the children together and give each child a number card. To begin the game, call out the names of two children. They must then stand up and show their number cards. Ask the whole group to read out the numbers shown and then ask them to add the two numbers together to obtain the total. Practise this process several times with different pairs of children to familiarize the group with the game. Once they understand the game and are confident to work independently, encourage the main body of the group to remain silent while the two children holding the cards work out the answer to their own sum. Reinforce correct answers by reiterating the sum: 'Well done! Two and three makes five. Excellent!'. If an incorrect answer is given, ask the children if they would like to count the dots on both cards just to make sure. Once the children become familiar with this game you may wish to record how long it takes for everybody in the group to have a turn and then try to beat this time on subsequent occasions.

Support

Use only number cards 1, 2 and 3 to begin with and do not introduce the time element until the children are secure in their recognition of the numbers and the process of addition.

Extension

This activity can be extended endlessly by using the larger numbers from the lower half of the photocopiable sheet and introducing other number operations such as subtraction, multiplication or even division.

HOME LINKS
Choose a 'number of the week' and ask parents to encourage their children to practise their addition skills by adding that amount to numbers that they notice in their environment. For example, if the number of the week is 2, then they must add 2 to house numbers that they pass, or the date on the calendar, or any other numbers that they spot.

MULTICULTURAL LINKS
Learn the numbers 1 to 5 in another language.

COUNTING AROUND

Learning objective
To count and order numbers.

What you need
The photocopiable sheet on page 73; coloured paper or card; scissors.

Preparation
Make two copies of the photocopiable sheet, each on a different colour and cut them up to make two sets of numbers from 1 to 10. (Laminate them for a lasting finish).

What to do
Using the first set of cards, give a number to ten children in the group. Then use the second set to give a number to each of the remaining children. (If the group consists of more than ten children but less than 20, ensure that you give out the second set in order so that there are no gaps in the sequence of numbers.)

Explain to the children that there are two sets of different-coloured cards and ensure that everyone knows which is which. Then tell them that you are going to play a counting game using one of the coloured sets of cards. Which number do they think should start the game? (Number one.) Ask the child holding the relevant colour number one to hold it up for everyone to see and call out 'One'. Which number comes next? (Two.) Again ask the relevant child to hold up the number and call it out. Once the children understand how to play, set them off with a 'Ready, steady, count!' and see how quickly they can count around the group with each child holding up their card and calling out the number in sequence. When the first set of number holders have had their turn, let the second set try the same thing.

Support
Use only the number cards 1 to 5 and let each child come to the front of the group as they call their number so that the sequence is visible to the remainder of the group as a prompt.

Extension
Shuffle the two sets of cards together before giving them out and challenge the group to count around using alternate colours, for example red 1, yellow 2, red 3, yellow 4 and so on. They could also try starting at a number other than one or counting in reverse order.

GROUP SIZE
Whole group.

WHERE IS IT?

Learning objective
To use everyday words to describe position.

What you need
Small object such as a pen or toy for each child; small cloth bag; the photocopiable sheet on page 74; thin card; scissors.

Preparation
Copy the photocopiable sheet onto thin card and cut up to make a starter set of position cards, laminating them for a durable finish.

What to do
Gather the children to sit in a circle and give each child a small object to hold. Look at the position cards together and talk about what each one means before putting them all into the bag. Explain that the children are each going to have a turn to put their object in a place shown by the cards and to do that they need to be able to count to, say, six. Then begin to pass the bag around the circle, counting as you go. When it gets to child number six, she dips her hand into the bag and withdraws a card, looks at it and places her object in a similar position to that shown. She then rejoins the circle and the game continues until all the objects are placed. The adult then asks each child in turn, 'Where did you put your toy?'. The child tries to remember and gives a reply, 'I put it behind the curtain'. He then looks behind the curtain, retrieves his toy (if it is there!) and returns to the circle. The game ends when all the children have retrieved their objects.

Support
Younger or less able children may need help to interpret the cards and encouragement or prompting to reply using the correct vocabulary.

Extension
Make a set of word cards rather than picture position cards and include such positions as opposite, to the left of and beneath.

HOME LINKS
Ask parents and carers to help their children to practise their positional vocabulary by hiding a small object and asking them to find it by guessing using positional language: 'Is it on the cupboard/behind the chair/between the table and the door?'.

MULTICULTURAL LINKS

Remember to include culturally diverse objects in your collection such as chopsticks, diva lamps and balti dishes.

I GUESS...

Learning objective
To practise making visual estimations of distance in footsteps.

What you need
Yourself and the children!

Preparation
Before attempting this game the children will need to have some experience of measuring by counting their steps.

What to do
Explain that you are going to play a guessing game that involves measuring and remind the children how to walk naturally while they count their steps, and to try not to take either huge 'giant steps' or tiny 'fairy steps'. Then start the game by choosing a place in the room and guessing how many steps it will take to get you there. Check it by measuring and if you are within one step either way stay there. If your estimate was not accurate return to your starting point. Choose a child to be the next player. The game continues until everybody has had a turn. Congratulate everyone who is in a different place from where they started because their estimations must have been accurate.

If time allows, let those children who are still at their starting point have another attempt in order to become more accurate. To vary the game on subsequent occasions, let each player set the destination for the following player and sometimes play the game outdoors to give it a different perspective.

Support
Suggest that shorter distances may be easier to estimate than longer ones and offer support to individual children by counting along with them as steps are taken towards the chosen object. Encourage the children to rethink estimates as they go along if they feel it necessary.

Extension
Challenge the children to estimate multiple distances such as the journey from the window, to the table, to the door, or set circuitous courses involving curves and bends.

GROUP SIZE
Up to ten children.

PUT THE LID ON

Learning objectives
To practise counting; to count reliably up to ten everyday objects.

What you need
Sets of four identical lidded containers such as margarine tubs or film canisters; plenty of different-sized objects.

Preparation
Ensure that you are in an area where the different-sized objects are accessible to the children.

What to do
Four children at a time can play the game while the remainder of the group slowly counts to 20 or 30 to set the time limit for the players. The object of the game is for each player to fill their container with a given number of objects and put its lid on within the set time.

Before the game begins, set rules for your own particular circumstances about where the children are allowed to search and where they are not. To start the game, give an identical container to each of four children and ask one of the remaining children to choose a number between five and ten. That number is the number of objects that each player must find to fit into his container before the group has finished counting. The game finishes either when a player fills his container and puts the lid on or when the group has counted to the required number. Check each player's container with the whole group and discuss whether it held more or less than the required amount, before choosing four more players for the next round of the game.

Support
Organize your playing area so that there are plenty of suitably-sized objects easily visible and readily accessible on table-tops and work with amounts of less than five.

Extension
Introduce extra rules for the collection of objects such as seven blue objects, nine round objects or eight items of different sizes.

HOME LINKS
Send the children home with a named and lidded film canister and challenge them to fill it with as many different small objects as possible such as a paper clip, piece of pasta or a sweet. Ask them to bring it back to the group the following week so that the items can be counted.

UPS AND DOWNS

Learning objective
To understand that heavier objects make one end of a balance go down.

What you need
A simple bucket or flat-bed balance; several small items of varying weights.

Preparation
Ensure that the group has had some prior experience of using balances in both free and structured play activities.

What to do
Gather the group together so that they all have a clear view of the balance. Talk about light and heavy objects and ask the children to recall what happens when two objects of different weights are placed on opposite ends of a balance. (One end goes up, the other goes down.) Is it the lighter or the heavier object that goes down? Consolidate this by demonstrating with two objects on the balance and reiterating, 'That's right, the heavier object goes down'.

Explain that you are going to play a game to see how clever the children are at finding objects that are heavier than yours and choose a child to play first. Select an item from those available and let the child feel its weight. Then put the item on the scales and challenge the child to find an item which is heavier than yours and which will make the other end of the balance go down. If the child is successful, congratulate him with reinforcing comments such as, 'Well done, your object was heavier, it made the balance go down!' Invite him to choose the next player. If the child is not successful commiserate with him and explain what went wrong: 'Oh dear, bad luck, your object wasn't heavy enough was it. It wouldn't make the balance go down, would it?'.

Support
Supply only a limited variety of objects that have large differences in their weight.

Extension
Introduce the term 'lighter' and set complex challenges such as finding objects which are 'heavier than the box but lighter than the doll'.

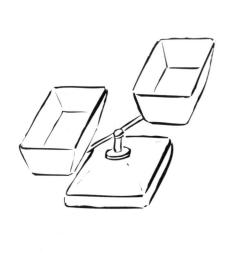

The natural world, the local environment and simple forces are focused upon in this chapter. The games incorporate a variety of stimulating resources to inspire and develop children's understanding of the world around them.

Knowledge and understanding of the world

FAMILY SNAP

Learning objective
To observe and identify features from the natural world.

What you need
A varied selection of real fruit and vegetables; two carrier bags.

Preparation
Gather the group together and look at each piece of fruit in turn. Talk about how and where it was grown, what it looks, feels and smells like and the fact that it belongs to the fruit family. Repeat the process with the vegetables, again emphasizing the fact that each is a member of the vegetable family.

What to do
Tell the children that you are going to play a game to see if they can remember which family each item belongs to. Invite two children to come to the front of the group and give each one a bag containing a selection of fruit and vegetables. Explain that the children are going to count to three, and on the count of three, the children at the front will dip their hands into their bags and take out a fruit or vegetable. The children must then look at the objects and decide whether they are members of the same family. If they are, they call out the appropriate family name – 'fruit' or 'vegetable' – but if not, they remain silent. After a few turns, let the original children return to the group and select two more children to take a turn at the front.

Vary the game by playing with other pairs of objects such as winter and summer clothes, pictures of animals and birds, or land and water vehicles.

Support
Before playing the game, play a simpler version by using two identical sets of three fruit. Ask the children to spot identical pairs as they are withdrawn and call out the names of the fruit – 'apple', 'orange' or 'pear'. Then play the game again using vegetables.

Extension
Invite three rather than two children to come to the front of the group, and use three different categories such as fruit, flowers and vegetables; animals, birds and insects; or land, water and air transport.

LET'S MAKE A BUTTERFLY

Learning objective
To identify some features of a living thing.

What you need
A dice; the photocopiable sheet on page 75; coloured pencils; poster or large photograph of a butterfly.

Preparation
Make a copy of the photocopiable sheet for each child. Look at the photograph of the butterfly and discuss it with the group, pointing out that the body is in three parts – the head, the thorax and the abdomen – and that there are four wings, two antennae and two eyes. Encourage the children to also notice that the butterfly's six legs are not visible when looked at from the top with its wings spread.

What to do
Explain that you are going to play a game to make a beautiful butterfly and that you will be using a dice to help you. Look at the photocopiable sheet together and again notice that the body is in three parts. There are four wings, two eyes and two antennae but no legs are visible. Point out that there are numbers written on the butterfly. What do the children think they are for? (To match with the dots on the dice.) Ask the children to explain how they think the game might be played, and then explain to them that each child takes it in turn to roll the dice and to colour in a part of the butterfly with the number that matches the dots. Play the game to find out who is lucky enough to be first to colour their complete butterfly.

Support
Use a dice with numbers to match rather than dots to count and allow the child to colour in all the relevant parts when a number is rolled, for example, four wings or two antennae or two eyes on one roll of the appropriate number.

Extension
Instead of using the photocopiable sheet ask the children to draw the relevant part of the butterfly on the roll of the dice. Encourage them to colour the wings symmetrically.

GROUP SIZE
Up to six children.

NATURAL TREASURE

Learning objective
To recognize and name various natural objects.

What you need
A carrier bag or other container for an adult to carry.

Preparation
NB Be aware that this activity may not be suitable for certain children at certain times of the year due to allergies, hay fever and asthma.

Tell the children that you are going to go outside and look for different things that are produced by nature. Discuss what these things might be and talk about the difference between natural and manufactured objects. Set the rules for where the children are allowed to go and which living things they are allowed to pick (probably just grasses and daisies).

What to do
Go outside with the children and begin to make your collection. Set a challenge for the children to see who can be first to find a really small stone or a really long blade of grass. Gradually make the challenge more difficult – perhaps there are shells or fossils to be found – talk about these as they are presented to you and suggest using books to find out more about them later. Remind the children not to pick anything that is growing without first checking with an adult, and not to touch or disturb any creatures that they spot. Accept all objects brought to you, but make a note of who found them first to use on a display later: 'Rakesh found the smallest stone', 'Claire found the longest piece of grass'.

After about five minutes, take your collection back indoors and make sure that everyone washes their hands thoroughly before coming to view the objects. Talk about what you have found and sort the things into their different groups, making a note to do some follow-up research into books if necessary. Keep some of the items to make a display, perhaps as a woven collage (see 'Wall of nature' on page 64). Press green items such as grasses and daisies between sheets of newspaper to preserve their shape and colour.

Support
Work with only two or three children at a time and restrict your hunting area by marking it out with chalks or ropes. Ask only for objects that are more easily found.

Extension
Challenge the children to sort and categorize the collection of items themselves and to make small information labels to go with their display.

HOME LINKS
Tell parents and carers that you would like to make a display of grasses and ask them to help their child find just two different types for your collection.

LAND, WATER OR AIR

Learning objective
To find out about and identify features from the natural world.

What you need
A large whiteboard and marker pen; a set of habitat cards (see Preparation).

Preparation
Make a set of 12 A5-sized cards comprising four with blue waves to represent water, four with a large cloud to represent the air and four with green hills to represent the land.

What to do
Gather the children together and look at the three different habitat cards together and explain that you are going to play a game that requires the children to tell you the names of different creatures that live in different places. Practise this now by asking, 'What lives on the land?' (squirrels, cats, dogs, horses, cows); 'What lives in the water?' (dolphins, whales, sharks, goldfish) and 'What lives in the air?' (blackbirds, owls, butterflies, wasps). Then shuffle together the cards and put them face down on a surface at the front of the group. Invite a child to turn the cards. Explain that as each card is turned, the children must name an appropriate animal for that habitat. The child holds up the first card and selects another child to answer. If the answer is correct, draw or write the name of the creature on the whiteboard, and the child who has answered can come out to turn the next card. The first child rejoins the group and the game continues. If a child names a creature already mentioned, he must try to think of a different one instead. At the end of the game, look at the list of creatures and count up how many were named altogether. Use this figure as your record and try to beat it the next time you play.

Support
Have pictures or posters of land, air and water creatures easily visible at the front of the group for reference.

Extension
Restrict the choice of creatures by imposing extra rules such as, 'The creatures today must all begin with the letter 's'' or 'Today's creatures must all be smaller than you!'.

WHAT SHALL I WEAR?

Learning objective
To select clothes to suit particular weather conditions.

What you need
The photocopiable sheet on page 76; thin card, a selection of clothing and accessories to suit all seasons – wellingtons, scarves, sun-hats, sandals, gloves.

Preparation
Make a dice for the game from thin card, using the net on the photocopiable sheet. **NB** The dice is a tetrahedron and therefore has only four faces – sun, rain, snow and a combination of all three. When the dice lands it should be picked up by its point, revealing its base to indicate the type of weather. It is designed this way so that all the players and the audience see the result at the same time.

What to do
Jumble all the clothes together on a table. Invite three children to dress up and designate each one to a particular type of weather. Show the children the types of weather shown on the dice – cold, wet and sunny – and explain that if the combination is thrown then all of the three children can choose an item to wear. Choose a child to roll the dice and read out the symbol shown. The appropriate child selects a suitable item and puts it on. The dice is rolled again and a piece of clothing selected by the appropriate child and so on. The game can continue until all available clothing has been used or until one child has put on four different items. The clothing is then checked piece by piece and if it is all correct the game is over. If an incorrect item is discovered, it is removed and the game continues until a child has put on four correct items.

Support
Keep the clothes in three separate, weather-related piles rather than mixing them all together.

Extension
Put all of the items into a bag and let the child select them by touch alone. Correctly chosen items can be put on but incorrectly chosen ones must be returned to the bag.

WHAT DOES THAT MEAN?

Learning objectives
To find out about and identify certain features of their environment; to understand and interpret familiar signs and symbols.

What you need
A Polaroid camera would be useful though not essential; pencils; paper; crayons.

Preparation
Familiarize yourself with the immediate surroundings both inside and outside your building, taking note of any signs or symbols such as zigzag lines on the road, fire hydrant signs, bus stops and 'children crossing'. Try to avoid too many written signs and concentrate on those with a more visual impact. Take photographs of them if possible.

What to do
Tell the children that you are going on a sign hunt and that they must try to spot as many signs as they can and try to remember what they look like so that they can draw them later. Then, take a short walk of only five minutes or so around your previously planned route, stopping at each sign that is spotted and having a very brief chat about each one as you go. Return to your setting and ask each child to recall just one of the signs that were seen and try to draw it. Finally, look at each child's sign and ask them to say a few words about where they saw it and what it is for.

Play this game on several occasions using different routes to build up a collection of the most important signs in your setting. Display the children's signs alongside any photographs that you have of the real thing.

Support
On your return from the walk, look at the photographs with the children and let them find the signs that they spotted and discuss them rather than draw them. Alternatively, if you have no photographs, ask the children to describe the signs to you, while you draw them for the children to talk about later.

Extension
Include some written signs on your route such as 'Entrance', 'Exit' and 'Reception' and encourage the children to write a few explanatory words of their own beneath their interpretation of the signs.

UPHILL RACERS

Learning objective
To investigate objects and materials.

What you need
Two strong magnets; two identical transparent plastic containers, two-thirds full of water; a collection of small, light, magnetic items such as paper clips, treasury tags, washers, screws and safety pins; aprons; sponge, mop and towel in case of accidents.

Preparation
Before you start this activity, test your equipment to ensure that the magnets are strong enough to enable the small objects to be pulled through the water and up the side of the container.

What to do
Divide the children into two teams and sit them in rows facing their plastic container of water on a waterproof table. Show them the magnets and the selection of objects and demonstrate how the objects are attracted to the magnet and will jump off your hand to get to it. Explain that this invisible force is called magnetism and that it can even travel through water. Again, demonstrate this by dropping a paper clip into one of the containers and using the magnet to slide it up the side of the container to the top. Then tell the children that they are going to play a game called 'Uphill racers' in which each child will have a turn to retrieve an object from the water using the magnet. Place a handful of the small objects into each container, ensuring that they are a small distance from each other, and give a magnet to one child in each team. Explain that this child should come to the front with the magnet and use it to retrieve an object from the water, before giving the magnet to the second child and moving to the back of his team. The second child then goes to the front, the rest of the team shuffles forward and the game continues. The game is over when each child in the team is holding a retrieved object and the team has returned to its starting position.

Support
Play the game with pairs of children instead of teams, letting the winner choose the next two players.

Extension
Make the task more difficult by adding some non-magnetic objects to the collection such as 5p coins, buttons, small balls of Plasticine or some small but heavy objects such as bolts. Suggest that each player must retrieve a different object to the previous player.

GROUP SIZE
Up to ten children.

DOWNHILL RACERS

Learning objective
To ask questions about why things happen and how things work.

What you need
Several identical small toy vehicles; two pieces of wood or strong card (approximately 50cm by 20cm); a safe indoor or outdoor space clear of obstacles (approximately 4m by 2m wide); chalk or pencil and paper.

Preparation
Ensure that the children have had prior experience of experimenting with toy vehicles on ramps and slopes.

What to do
Explain that you are going to play 'Downhill racers' but that the winner of each race will be the vehicle that travels the furthest, not the one that finishes first. Show the children the pieces of wood and demonstrate how to keep one end on the ground and raise or lower the other end to make slopes of varying steepness. Tell the children that they must hold their vehicle in the starting position and release it when you give the signal. Remind them that they must just let go of the vehicle and should not push it in any way, but that they can alter their slope if they wish. Choose two children to start the game. When the two vehicles have stopped moving, decide which is ahead and mark the spot with the child's name using chalk or record it on paper. The next two players take their turn and if either goes beyond the existing marker, mark the spot with the new leader's name. The game continues until everybody has had at least one turn and the overall champion is congratulated.

Support
Let the children use a few wooden bricks to support their slope rather than trying to hold it with one hand while releasing their vehicle with the other.

Extension
Use a tape measure and a large protractor to record distances against slopes to see if steepness makes any significant difference to distance.

HOME LINKS
Encourage the children to continue their experiments at home using balls or cardboard cylinders and to see what happens when they try rolling them up as well as down different slopes.

WHAT'S IT MADE OF?

Learning objective
To find out about and identify some features of different objects.

What you need
A wooden board; a plastic bowl; an old coffee or powdered milk tin (leave the lid on for safety reasons); a selection of small everyday items made of wood, metal or plastic (at least one for each child); a box or bag to put them in.

Preparation
Gather the group together and look at the board, the bowl and the tin, in turn. Let the children pass each object around as it is discussed and feel whether it is warm or cold, hard or soft, rigid or pliable. Suggest that they tap it to see how it sounds. Compare the items and their properties with one another before asking the group to say what they think each item is made of.

What to do
Sit the children in a circle around the board, the bowl and the tin and show them the box of objects. Explain that you are going to pass the box around the circle and that as it passes, each child should select an object and take it out of the box. When every child has an object, put the box to one side and invite a child to start the game. He must hold up his chosen object for all to see and tell the group what it is and what he thinks it is made of. If he is correct, he places his object on the appropriate item in the centre of the circle and chooses someone else to continue the game. If he is incorrect, ask him if he would like to compare his item with the three in the middle and see if he can find the one that it feels and sounds like. Continue the game until everyone has had a turn.

Finally, look at the assembled items in the centre of the circle and ask the group to remind you what each set is made of.

Support
Let younger and less able children use only wood and metal items.

Extension
Make the task more difficult by including in the box items made from a mixture of two or more of the materials and asking for ideas on how they might be sorted.

GROUP SIZE
Up to eight
children.

GUESS WHERE I'VE BEEN!

Learning objective
To find out and talk about features of their environment.

What you need
A shopping bag or basket; several sets of objects depicting a particular place in the local environment, for example a parcel, some stamps and a letter (post office); costume and towel (swimming-pool); fruit and vegetables (greengrocer's); purse, timetable and ticket (bus station).

Preparation
Put up a screen and place your sets of objects behind it, out of view of the children.

What to do
Show the children your empty bag or basket and tell them that you are going to go on a little journey and when you come back they must try to guess where you have been by looking at the things in your bag. Go for a little walk among the children, talking to yourself as you go: 'Hmm, I wonder where I shall go today? Do I need any shopping? Is there a special place I would like to visit? Hmm, I wonder…'. Disappear behind the screen and place your chosen set of objects in your bag before coming back into view of the children.

Take the objects one by one from your bag and invite the group to suggest where you might have been. When they have made a correct guess, ask them what else you might have put in your bag for clues or ask them if they have ever visited that particular place and what they did there. Continue the game either by going on another trip yourself or by inviting a child to take over from you.

HOME LINKS
Invite parents and carers to accompany you on a walk around the local area to look at various shops and other establishments.

MULTICULTURAL LINKS
Remember to include items from all cultures served by your local community – bowls and chopsticks from a local Chinese restaurant or sari material and henna powder from Asian shops.

Support
Ask the child taking over from you to whisper their destination to you and accompany them behind the screen to help them decide which items to put in their bag.

Extension
Remove items from your bag one by one, allowing time for guessing to take place before showing the next item.

CHAPTER 5

Physical development

Children's ability to move with control and to express themselves through movement is developed in this chapter. The games provide opportunities to observe and recreate movements, to use a balloon to practise hand-eye co-ordination and to follow directional instructions.

GROUP SIZE
Whole group.

HOME LINKS
Give each child a copy of the photocopiable sheet to complete at home to remind them of their various body parts.

MULTICULTURAL LINKS
Use this game to teach the children two or three of the major body parts in a language other than English.

CEILING, FLOOR, WINDOW, DOOR

Learning objectives
To move with control and co-ordination; to show awareness of space and others.

What you need
Space for the children to stretch and spread their limbs; the photocopiable sheet on page 77.

Preparation
Ensure that the children know the names of their major body parts – head, hand, arm, elbow, shoulder, leg, knee and foot. Make a copy of the photocopiable sheet for each child.

What to do
Spend a minute or two practising pointing to the floor, ceiling, window and door on command. Then chant the following rhyme together as you do the actions:
'Point to the ceiling, point to the floor.
Point to the window, point to the door.'
Tell the children that you are going to play a game using that rhyme, but instead of pointing to the floor or ceiling, they are going to listen carefully to find out which part of their body they should stretch towards the ceiling, floor, window or door. Suggest that the children spread out into a space of their own and remind them to be careful not to bump into anybody else. Chant the rhyme again, this time replacing 'point' with a part of the body: 'Elbow to the ceiling, elbow to the floor. Elbow to the window, elbow to the door'.
Encourage the children to really stretch, and to remember to give both elbows a turn. Continue the game using different parts of the body for as long as the children remain interested. Finish by standing up and giving each limb in turn a gentle shake to loosen it up.

Support
Encourage younger or less able children to join in by performing the actions yourself with enthusiasm at the front of the group.

Extension
Let the children work in pairs, joining both hands with their partners and include the less familiar body parts such as heel, ankle, wrist and hip.

GROUP SIZE
Whole group.

LET'S GO

Learning objective
To move with confidence and imagination.

What you need
A space large enough for the children to move around safely.

What to do
Gather the children together and explain that you are going to play a follow-the-leader game. Does anybody know what that means? Talk about the idea of following one after the other in a long line and trying to imitate the movement of the person at the front. Practise this a few times with yourself as leader. Make sure you choose simple movements such as walking on tiptoe or creeping on hands and feet, and begin each journey by saying what you intend to do: 'Hmm! I think this time we will all... take big giant steps around the room. Are you ready? Then let's go!'. Finish each journey back at the starting point.

Once the children are confident, invite a child to think of a movement to do, then let them take up their position at the front of the line. Encourage them to tell the rest of the group how they are going to move and ask them to say, 'Let's go!' when they intend to start. When they are back at the start, the leader goes to the back of the line and the new leader takes up their position. Continue the game until all the children who want to have had at least one turn each and finish by gathering the group together and recalling some of the different ways that they have moved.

Support
Younger children, although eager to be leaders, may find it difficult to come up with ideas for moving, so be ready to offer two or three alternatives for them to choose from.

Extension
Encourage older children to invent sequences of movements rather than simple repetitions. For example, hop, hop, jump; hop, hop, jump or step, turn, step; step, turn, step. Suggest that they could use their whole body, not just their feet.

HOME LINKS
Tell parents and carers that you have been thinking about different ways of moving. Encourage them to continue this at home with their children by seeing how many different ways they can find of travelling from their front gate to their front door, or across their lounge or down their garden.

GROUP SIZE
Whole group.

I SENT A POSTCARD TO MY FRIEND

Learning objective
To move with control and co-ordination.

What you need
A large open space suitable for both sitting and running; the photocopiable sheet on page 78.

Preparation
Learn the following rhyme with the children:
'I sent a postcard to my friend and on the way I dropped it.
One of you has picked it up and put it in your pocket.
It is you, it isn't you; it is you, it isn't you.'
Copy the photocopiable sheet for each child and one for yourself. Make a postcard by drawing in a picture and filling in who it is to and from with question marks. Cut along the lines and fold it in half before gluing it closed. Laminate your postcard to make it more durable.

What to do
Gather the children together in a circle and explain that you are going to play a racing game and that the children will need to be able to run very fast. Suggest that you have a practice to show them what you mean.

Show the children your completed postcard and begin to chant the memorized rhyme as you walk around the circle. When you come to the last line, slow down and say, 'It *is* you' or 'It *isn't* you' between adjacent pairs of children, repeating the lines as often as you like until on your final 'It *is* you' you place the postcard on the floor between two children. Tell those two children to stand up and face each other. Explain that they are going to race around the circle in opposite directions and back to their places on the floor. The first child sitting with legs crossed and arms folded will be the winner. Remind them to look where they are going as they run so as not to crash into each other halfway around the circle. The winner takes the postcard and the game continues for as long as desired.

Support
It is safer for very young children to race around the circle in the same direction as each other.

Extension
Vary the game by using different ways of racing around the circle, such as on hands and feet, hopping, skipping or jumping.

HOME LINKS
Show the children the photocopiable sheet and your completed postcard as an example. Ask them to write their own name and a friend's in the 'To' and 'From' sections. Then give each child a copy of the photocopiable sheet to take home and suggest that they bring back their completed card to deliver it to their friend in the group.

GROUP SIZE
Six to eight children.

VOLLEY-BALLOON

Learning objective
To enjoy working and playing as part of a team.

What you need
Balloons; a length of ribbon or transparent material and a means of securing it across the playing area as a net (use two adult helpers if secure fixings are not available); a box.

Preparation
Inflate several balloons and keep them in a box until needed.

What to do
Gather the children together and explain that you are going to play a game with balloons called volley-balloon. Tell the children that the object of the game is to keep the balloon from touching the floor but that players must use only their hands to touch the balloon.

Divide the group into two teams and give each team a balloon. Let them practise patting the balloon to one another without letting it drop to the floor. Remind the children that hands only must be used and that they must take turns to pat the balloon.

Put away one of the balloons and erect the net at about child head height. Explain that they must now take turns to pat the balloon back and forth over the net to their opponents, trying not to let the balloon touch the floor. Set a time limit for the game, and during that time count how many times the balloon touches the floor. Make a note of the total and try to reduce it during subsequent games.

Support
Mark a line on the floor to divide the playing area into two halves rather than using a net or let the children work in pairs rather than teams.

Extension
As the children become more skilled introduce a simple scoring system – if the balloon touches the floor in your half of the area your opponents score one point – and use teams of up to six children.

HOME LINKS
Tell parents and carers you have been playing a simplified version of volleyball using balloons and ask them to play other throwing and catching games with their children using balloons, beanbags, sponges and other light objects.

WAKE UP, MUM!

Learning objective
To move in a quiet and controlled way.

What you need
A bunch of keys; a chair.

What to do
Arrange the children in a line and place the chair in front, facing away from the children at a distance of about three metres. Invite a child to be 'Mum' (or 'Dad') and to sit on the chair at the front of the group. Give the child the bunch of keys to put under the chair and then ask her to close her eyes and pretend to be asleep until the children tell her to wake up. While she sleeps, select a child from the line to creep as quietly as possible, pick up the keys without a sound and return to their place hiding the keys behind their back. (Remind all of the children to keep their hands behind their back so as not to give the game away.)

All of the children then chant, 'Wake up Mum! Someone's stolen your keys!'. Mum wakes up, turns around and scans the line of children to try to detect who has the keys. If she identifies the holder of the keys correctly she chooses someone else to be Mum (or Dad if it's a boy of course). If she is incorrect then the holder of the keys is automatically Mum. The game continues until everyone has had a turn either to be Mum or to take the keys.

Support
Younger children may find it difficult to hold the keys behind their backs. Suggest that they lie them on the floor behind them so that Mum cannot see them. All of the children can then keep their hands in their laps.

Extension
Suggest that the children stand very close together and carefully pass the keys up and down the line behind their backs (or just pretend to do so!), while Mum is watching them and trying to decide which child is holding the keys.

OVER AND UNDER

Learning objective
To travel in a variety of ways.

What you need
A large open area where children can move safely.

What to do
Spend a few moments talking about bridges – what they are and what their function is. Then ask the children to make a bridge of their own using their body. Encourage them to think of as many different sorts of bridges as they can and to try to use all the different parts of their body. Can they make a wide bridge? A high bridge? Can they hold their bridge shape while you count slowly to ten?

Divide the group into two halves and ask one half to make really strong bridges while the other half travels about the room on hands and feet trying to go under all the bridges. Then change over and let the first half travel around while the second half make the bridges. Repeat the process, but this time tell the children who are being bridges that once someone has passed under them they must lie down, thus making them inaccessible to other travellers. Tell the travellers that once they have been under one bridge, they too should lie down. The game finishes when all the children are lying down. If you have time, play the game again so that all the children will have had a turn to be both traveller and bridge.

Support
Spend a lot of time practising making strong bridges to ensure that the children really can sustain them long enough for another child to pass underneath before moving on to the actual game.

Extension
Let the children work in pairs to make bridges or consider timing the game to find out which half of the group can pass under all the bridges in the shortest amount of time.

GROUP SIZE
Two teams of up to
six children.

PASS IT ON

Learning objective
To handle objects safely and with increasing control.

What you need
A large soft ball for each team.

What to do
Gather all of the children together into a long line and explain that you are going to race to pass a ball back between your legs to the person behind you. Stand at the front of the line and demonstrate by holding one of the balls in a secure two-handed grip and passing it back through your legs to the child behind you. Encourage the children to continue to pass the ball back through their legs to the child behind, reminding them to hold the ball with two hands so that it doesn't drop to the floor. When the ball arrives at the last child, tell her to run quickly to the front of the line ready to start all over again. Practise this a couple of times until you are sure that the children are confident about what to do. Then divide the children into two equal teams and give a ball to the child at the front of each line. Explain that as soon as you say, 'Go!', they must start to pass the ball through their legs. Do they remember what the child at the end of the line has to do when the ball arrives? (Run to the front.)

As soon as everyone has had a turn at the front of the line and the original leader is back in position at the front, he should hold the ball high above his head so that you will know that his team has finished and you can declare them the winners.

Support
Use a medium-sized sponge ball with very young children as they may have difficulty fitting a larger one through their legs without losing their balance.

Extension
Repeat the activity, passing the ball overhead rather than through the legs or complicate it further by passing it alternately under and over down the line.

HOME LINKS
Encourage parents
and carers to help
their children to
think of other relays
that could be played
using just a ball and
try them out during
a future session.

GROUP SIZE
Whole group.

HOP, STEP AND JUMP

Learning objective
To follow directional instructions.

What you need
Nine sheets of A4 card; felt-tipped pens; chalk or lengths of white tape.

Preparation
Write 'hop', 'step', and 'jump' on three cards; '1', '2', and '3' on three more and on the remaining three, draw a large arrow pointing upwards with the word 'forwards' written above it, one pointing down with 'backwards' under it and a cross with 'on the spot' written alongside. Mark a series of parallel lines on the playing surface, making them between five and ten metres long depending on the area available.

What to do
Show the children each action card in turn and practise hopping, stepping and jumping for a few moments to ensure that the children know what each action requires. Then show them the arrow cards and talk about what they mean.

Finally, look at the number cards together and practise hopping, stepping or jumping the appropriate number of times for each card.

To play the game, choose three children to each hold a set of cards and spread out the remaining children along the first line so that the other lines lie before them like a ladder. Explain that the children must try to follow the instructions shown on the cards that the three children facing them will hold up.

Ask the child with the action cards, 'What are we going to do, Hannah?' and help the children to interpret the card she holds up: 'Hmm! We're going to hop'. Then ask the direction cardholder, 'Which way are we going, Sundip?' and again interpret the direction: 'Okay, we're going backwards. We are going to hop backwards'. Finally, ask, 'And how many lines are we going to hop over, Teri? Three! Wow that's going to be difficult! We're going to hop backwards over three lines. Let's go!'.

Continue playing the game for as long as desired, remembering to change the cardholders over every few minutes to give others a turn. Finish the game by recalling what you have been doing and hopping, jumping or skipping from one end of the ladder to the other.

Support
Dispense with the directional cards and the lines and just hop, step or jump the appropriate number of times into a space within the playing area.

Extension
Add 'left' and 'right' arrows to the set and use a grid rather than the set of parallel lines, eliminating any child who goes beyond it.

HOME LINKS
Encourage parents and carers to play board games such as Snakes and Ladders with their children so that they can practise moving counters forwards and backwards on a track or grid.

GROUP SIZE
Whole group.

LISTEN AND MOVE

Learning objective
To use musical cues to move in different ways.

What you need
One or more percussion instruments such as a drum, a shaker, a scraper or a tambourine.

Preparation
Gather the children into a circle and pass the instruments around to let everyone produce at least one sound from it. Help the children to notice the different sounds that are being created.

What to do
Pick out three or four distinct sounds that the instruments can produce and tell the children that you think it is telling you how it wants you to move. Listen to the first sound together and decide which movement it is suggesting – it might be running, creeping, marching, jumping or suddenly standing as still as a statue. Choose two or three more sounds and decide on their accompanying movement, practising a few times to make sure that the children know what each sound means. Explain that you are going to play a game in which the children must listen very carefully to hear what the instrument is telling them to do. Sometimes they will have to run, sometimes tiptoe and sometimes stand very still, but all of the time they must listen because if anyone forgets to do what the instrument tells them, they will be out of the game. Then begin playing the sounds and watch carefully so as to eliminate any children who do not change their movements to match the instrument. When someone is eliminated, enlist their help to spot others who are slow to respond to the music.

The game ends when there are just two children left. Suggest that they shake hands and congratulate each other on their success.

Support
Set a time limit for the game rather than playing it as an elimination.

Extension
Use a different instrument for each action and ask children to be musicians. Encourage them to decide among themselves who is going to play their instrument next and for how long it will be played. Suggest that they play behind a screen so that the group has only aural clues to help them.

HOME LINKS
Ask parents and carers to listen to some instrumental music with their children and see if they can pick out different sounds made by the instruments playing.

MULTICULTURAL LINKS
Each time you play this game, use an instrument from a different country or culture.

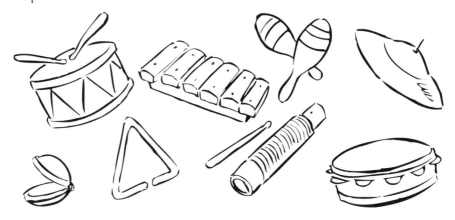

GROUP SIZE
Up to ten children.

DRIBBLE AND TRAP

Learning objective
To direct an object with increasing control.

What you need
A medium-sized ball (about 10cm to15cm in diameter) for each child.

Preparation
Ensure that the children have had some practise at dribbling a ball.

What to do

Space the children out around the room and ask them to sit cross-legged on the floor. Give each child a ball and ask them to keep it safely contained in their laps. Explain that a ball always seems to want to get away from people, but that the children are going to learn not to let it! Demonstrate how to gently tap the ball with the inside of the foot to move it along the ground trapping it with the sole of the foot to stop it if it tries to go too fast and get away. Let the children practise this for a few moments before starting the game. Remind them that they must use only their feet, not their hands.

Tell the children that you are going to play a game called 'Dribble and trap', and remind them that their ball will be trying to get away from them all of the time, but they must not let it or their ball will win the game. Explain that they are going to dribble and trap their ball all over the playing area and that you are going to watch carefully. If you spot any balls that are getting away you will trap them yourself and award one point to the ball! When you have trapped ten balls the game will be over and the balls will have won. However, if you run out of time before trapping that many balls, then the children will have won. Each time you trap a ball remind everyone of the score and tell them to be extra vigilant because the balls are getting to be very clever and might win the game.

Support
Work with groups of up to only six with very young children.

Extension
Use larger balls and ask a child to take over your task of trapping the balls that get away and awarding points.

HOME LINKS
Ask parents and carers to reinforce the idea of dribbling and trapping at home by encouraging their children to try the game with smaller balls using their hands.

The activities in this chapter will inspire children to think creatively and to develop confidence in their own ideas. They are provided with opportunities to work as a team, to produce a textural collage, to share their knowledge of simple songs and to form imaginative ideas around an unusual object.

Creative development

GROUP SIZE
Whole group.

HOME LINKS
Suggest to the children that they play this game at home with other members of the family and invite them to bring some of the results back to share with the group.

WHAT CAN IT BE?

Learning objective
To explore shape and form in two dimensions.

What you need
Blank flip chart or large sheets of paper; two different-coloured pens.

Preparation
Ensure that the children have had plenty of practice at free drawing.

What to do
Place the flip chart in full view of the group and draw a simple line with one of the pens. Stand back to allow the children a clear view of the line and ask them to tell you what the picture might be when it is finished. Take up one of their suggestions and, using the other pen, draw extra lines to complete the picture. Using the first pen, copy the original line and take up another suggestion and again complete the drawing using the second pen. Repeat the process until you have several different pictures all derived from the same first line. Look at the results with the group and point out that the pictures are all very different but that they all started off the same. Trace over the original line with your finger to emphasize this fact.

Flip over to the next page and draw a different starting line. Again ask the group to suggest ideas but this time invite those with suggestions to come to the front one by one to complete the picture themselves. Ensure that they use the second, different-coloured pen, so that the original line remains clearly visible.

Support
Draw very simple lines that can easily be made into everyday objects such as an arch that could become an umbrella, rainbow or bridge; or a circle that could become a face, flower or ball. If the children still seem unsure, give verbal clues and hints such as, 'Hmm, that shape reminds me of something that I use when it's raining!'.

Extension
Ask the child converting the line into a picture to do so without telling anyone what he is thinking so that the rest of the children can try to guess what it is. Alternatively, invite older children to play the game in pairs, each taking turns to draw a line for the other to convert.

NAME THAT TUNE

Learning objective
To recognize and sing simple songs from memory.

What you need
A quiet area.

Preparation
Ensure that the children are already familiar with a wide range of songs and rhymes.

What to do
Gather the children together in a quiet corner suitable for careful listening and where you will not disturb anyone else. Tell the children that you are going to hum the pattern of a song or rhyme that they have sung lots of times before, and that they must listen very carefully and try to guess

what that song is without hearing any of its words. For the first few songs, hum reasonably tunefully to help the children to identify the song and encourage them to join in with you when they know what it is.

Once the children are familiar with the game, begin to hum the rhythm using only a little variation in tone. When they have had plenty of practice, clap the rhythm or tap it out on a drum or other percussion instrument. Once each song or rhyme has been identified, sing it through completely with the children as you clap or tap out the rhythm to help those who are finding it difficult. Encourage the children to clap the rhythm with you.

Support
Mouth the words as you tap the rhythm to give visual as well as aural clues to very young or musically inexperienced children.

Extension
Encourage older children to take turns themselves to hum, clap or tap out rhythms for the rest of the group to identify.

GROUP SIZE
Whole group.

I CAN SHOW OFF

Learning objective
To express and communicate their ideas using dance, songs or musical instruments.

What you need
No special equipment is necessary, though a microphone would give an added dimension to the activity and a few simple percussion instruments might come in useful.

Preparation
If you plan to use a microphone, let the children have a little practice at using it before the show.

What to do
Explain that you would like to stage a little concert or show but that you don't have any singers or dancers to perform. Could the children help out? Is there anyone who knows a dance that they could show to the rest of the group, or someone who could sing or play a tune? When you have chosen a child, ask them to tell you a little bit about what they are going to do. If it is a dance, do they need a lot of space? Ask them where they learned the dance or did they make it up themselves? If it is a song, do they want the rest of the group to sing along with them if they know it, or do they want them just to listen? Would they like to use the microphone? Suggest that when they have finished their performance they bow to the audience. (Demonstrate this if necessary.)

Using the microphone if you have one, introduce the act to the audience: 'And now girls and boys we have Miss Samina Lam who is going to perform a dance that she has learned at Miss Sue's dancing academy'. When the performance is over, lead the audience in a round of applause and thank the 'artiste' enthusiastically: 'Thank you Miss Lam, that was beautifully performed. Please take a seat with the audience and enjoy the rest of the show'. Ask if another child would like to perform a different act and continue as before.

HOME LINKS
Make this activity a regular part of your sessions for a few weeks to make sure that everyone who wants to gets a chance to perform. Ask parents and carers to help their children to learn a song, dance, rhyme or simple magic trick to perform to the group.

Support
Offer to accompany the performer 'on stage' or ask them if they would like to be accompanied by a friend to boost their confidence.

Extension
Invite a child to host the show and introduce the acts.

GROUP SIZE
Whole group.

LET'S MAKE A WALL PICTURE

Learning objective
To explore colour, shape and space in two dimensions.

What you need
A piece of plastic sheeting about 1m by 1.5m; coloured paper; card in various colours; Blu-Tack or similar; a cardboard box covered over with a piece of fabric.

Preparation
Decide on a theme for the picture (an underwater scene perhaps) and cut out suitable shapes from the coloured card (fish, seaweed, shells, octopus), making sure that there is at least one shape for each child. Place the shapes in the box. Fix the large sheet of plastic onto a vertical surface (a wall or two painting easels side by side) at the children's working height.

What to do
Gather the children together to sit facing the blank plastic. Explain to the children that they are going to work together to make a big picture for the wall (of an underwater scene). Show them some of the shapes from the box and explain that each child will have a chance to feel under the fabric into the box and select a shape to add to the picture. Demonstrate how to use small pieces of Blu-Tack to hold a shape in place on the paper.

Invite the first child to dip a hand into the box to find a shape. Remind the rest of the group that they must watch carefully and offer advice if someone inadvertently places their shape upside-down or back to front. Once the first child has attached his shape in position with Blu-Tack, he chooses someone else to select and position a shape. The game continues until everyone has had a turn. Then look at the picture together and decide whether any of the components need moving or whether the picture is fine as it is. Display the picture for a day or two before carefully dismantling it and saving the cut-out shapes either for use again in another temporary group collage or for use in individual collage work.

Support
Let the children choose their shape rather than take pot luck from the covered box.

Extension
Suggest that individual children might wish to return to the collage later with pens or paints to add further detail.

GROUP SIZE
Whole group.

HOME LINKS
Ask parents and carers to bring in any interesting materials that could be used for collage work (off-cuts of ribbon or braid, shredded paper packaging, wood shavings).

TILES AND MORE TILES

Learning objective
To explore pattern and form in two dimensions.

What you need
The photocopiable sheet on page 79; thin card.

Preparation
Enlarge the photocopiable sheet to A3 size and copy onto thin card – enough for one between two children – and cut along the lines to make two sets of ten tiles, five grey and five half grey/half white. Make several copies of the photocopiable sheet for yourself and use the resulting sets of tiles to make a selection of patterns based on a 3 x 3 square. (Some ideas for this are given on the photocopiable sheet.) **NB** Reverse the grey tiles to get white ones.

What to do
Give each child a set of ten tiles and lead them to discover that there are three types – all grey, all white (the reverse of the grey) and half grey/half white. Explain that the tiles can be used to make lots of different patterns by placing them in different positions. Allow a few moments for the children to experiment with the tiles for themselves before calling their attention to the patterns that you have made previously. Look at one of your patterns and count how many tiles were used to create it. How many grey tiles were used? How many white? How many grey/white? Work through the pattern systematically from left to right and from top to bottom, inviting the children to find the relevant tiles in their set and copy your pattern tile by tile.

Ask the children to jumble up their tiles and start all over again, this time with no help from you! Ask them to raise their hand and call, 'Tiles!' when they have finished. Check the caller's pattern and if it is correct, let her choose which of your patterns the group should try next. If incorrect, ask her to check it again while the rest of the group carries on trying to be first to finish.

Support
Use patterns based on a 2 x 2 square and let the children help each other rather than race against each other.

Extension
Give each child a set of twenty tiles and use patterns based on a 4 x 4 square.

WALL OF NATURE

Learning objectives
To respond in a variety of ways to what they see and touch; to explore colour, texture and shape in three dimensions.

What you need
A piece of netting or open-weave fabric; two canes or thin twigs as long as the width of the fabric; needle and thread for adult use; a collection from the children of grasses, leaves, daisies, buttercups, feathers and other natural products or use the materials gathered during the activity 'Natural treasure' on page 41 of Chapter 4 (**NB** Ensure that the children do not bring in protected items such as shells and remind them not to pick wild flowers); a book of raffle tickets; a small box or bucket.

Preparation
Use the needle and thread to attach one cane to the top and one to the bottom of the fabric and hang it against a wall at the children's working height. Sort through the collection of items, discarding any that may be sharp, splintery or dangerous in any way. Arrange them in a row on a surface close to the wall hanging. Place a raffle ticket

above each item then fold its matching stub in half and place it in the bucket. **NB** Check that none of the children suffer from hay fever.

What to do
Gather the group together facing the suspended fabric. Explain that you are going to work together to make a wall hanging by weaving the assembled items in and out of the material to hold them in place. Demonstrate how this can be done horizontally, vertically or diagonally.

Invite two or three children to come to the front to dip into the bucket, withdraw a ticket and find the item with the matching number and weave it into the fabric. The game continues until all of the children have had at least one turn each and there are no more items to thread. Look at and admire the finished hanging together and explain that it will be left on the wall for everyone to see. Tell them that it can be worked and reworked as often as the children want to because each piece is not permanently fixed and so can be moved as desired to different positions for different effects. Remind the children to wash their hands every time they finish handling the wall hanging.

Support
Use very openly-woven fabric and ensure that your collection contains plenty of easy-to-weave items such as long grasses, pieces of straw and long-stemmed daisies.

Extension
Impose rules for the placing of the items such as, 'each one should be placed at a different angle to the previous one'; 'each one should be close to but not overlapping the last' and 'no item must be placed next to a similar one'.

FUN WITH COLOURS

Learning objective
To explore colour in two dimensions.

What you need
For every four to six children you will need: a table and chairs; a dice; six different-coloured pencil crayons; a copy of the photocopiable sheet on page 80 for each child.

Preparation
Number each set of pencil crayons 1 to 6 and place one set alongside a dice in the centre of each table.

What to do
Sit the children around the tables in groups of four to six and explain that you are going to play a colouring game. Draw the children's attention to the dice and the numbers on the pencil crayons in the centre of the table. Show them the colouring sheet and ask them how they think the colouring game might be played. If no suitable ideas are forthcoming, lead them to discover that they must take turns to roll the dice and then select the crayon with the matching number. That child then colours in just one section of their sheet and the next child rolls the dice.

When everyone appears to understand the game, give each child a colouring sheet and play the game until everyone has completed their picture. Look at some of the results together and remind the children that although they all started with identical sheets, they look very different now. Suggest that you might play again sometime to see how many more different results you can get.

Support
Use a dice with colours instead of numbers and at least two crayons of each colour so that two children can be colouring at once. Have an adult at each table to remind the children to colour only one section at each throw of the dice.

Extension
Add a rule stating that no two adjoining sections must be the same colour. Alternatively, instead of using six different colours, use six different patterns, such as stripes, spots, zigzags, checks, concentric lines and parallel wavy lines.

GROUP SIZE
Up to ten children.

I THINK IT COULD BE...

Learning objectives

To express and communicate their ideas in response to a range of materials; to respond in a variety of imaginative ways to what they see and touch.

What you need

Unusual or non-specific objects, or parts of objects, such as a rubber seal from a pressure cooker, the element from an old kettle or an old spool from an industrial knitting machine; a piece of fabric or a box.

What to do

Keep the objects in the box or hidden under the fabric until it is time to introduce one of them to the children. Explain that you have found something that you want to show to the group. Say that you are sure it is something very special but you have no idea what it is or what it might be for and you would like the children's help in deciding. Select one of your objects, putting the others to one side for a future game. Pass it around the group and encourage each child to explore the object and suggest how it might be used or what its purpose might be. The ideas can be as bizarre as the children make them – the rubber seal could be an elephant's wedding ring or a pig's necklace and the spool could be a pirate's false leg or a lightweight traffic bollard! Talk about the practicalities of their ideas. How might elephants wear their wedding ring since they have no fingers? Would the spool be suitable for any size pirate? If not, how might it be adapted to fit?

Finish the game by briefly recalling and counting all of the ideas that have come up. Consider recording them to make an illustrated 'Ideas book' at a later date.

Support

Encourage very young children to demonstrate how to use the object if they are having difficulty explaining it in words.

Extension

Suggest that older children draw a large picture showing how they think the object might be used and display the results around the actual object.

HOME LINKS
Explain to parents and carers that you have been encouraging the children to think imaginatively. Suggest that they continue this at home by writing down any story that their children might tell and encouraging them to illustrate it.

MULTICULTURAL LINKS
Look out constantly for objects from other lands and cultures to add to your collection. (Unusual items can often be found in charity shops, thereby keeping costs to a minimum.)

GROUP SIZE
Up to ten children.

WHAT NO PAINT?

Learning objective

To respond in a variety of ways to what they see; to use a widening range of materials in designing and making.

What you need

A large outdoor area with a light-coloured surface such as paving slabs; one or two buckets of water; two or three balls of different sizes.

Preparation

This activity can become rather messy and needs to take place on a warm, dry day. You may also feel it necessary to protect the children with waterproof aprons and wellington boots.

What to do

Ask the children to hold hands to form a circle and then slowly shuffle backwards until their arms are at almost full stretch. Then tell them to stand very still and let go hands, thus keeping well-spaced around the circle. Explain that you are going to paint a large water-picture on the ground by bouncing or rolling balls back and forth across the circle to each other. Invite a child to begin the game and ask her to choose a ball and dip it into the water before returning to her place in the circle. Tell her to choose a friend across the circle from her and to call out that friend's name before rolling or bouncing the ball carefully to her. Talk about the pattern the ball has made as it crossed the circle and encourage subsequent players to try to make different patterns. When the ball has become too dry to leave a trail, invite the next player to either wet it again or choose a different ball to dip into the water.

   At the end of the game, stand and watch the pattern for a few moments and talk about what is happening and why. (The pattern is changing because parts of it are beginning to dry out.)

Support

Demonstrate to very young children how to do a two-handed chest pass to bounce the ball accurately, and to squat and use both hands when rolling the ball.

Extension

Place heavy obstacles on the surface and challenge the children to pass the ball to a neighbouring child by ricocheting it off an obstacle.

HOME LINKS
Ask parents to donate old, clean paintbrushes of varying sizes for the group to use for further water-painting activities.

GROUP SIZE
Up to ten children.

PASS THE PLAY DOUGH

Learning objectives
To respond in a variety of ways to what they touch; to use their imagination in art.

What you need
A small ball of soft, pliable play dough, a large one-minute sand-timer or a kitchen-timer.

Preparation
Ensure that all of the children have had plenty of experience of using play dough.

What to do
Gather the children into a circle and show them the ball of play dough and the timer. Demonstrate how the dough can be manipulated quickly and simply into different shapes to make a face, a bowl, a flower and many other everyday objects. Explain that you are going to play a game to see how many different objects you can create between you. Tell them that when it is their turn with the dough, each child will have just one minute to turn the dough into something different.

To start the game, give the dough to any child to pass around the circle and count until it gets to the third child, who then has one minute to create and name an object. Admire the object: 'What a wonderful saucepan! That was an excellent idea. Well done!'. Remind the children that the next player must make something different with the dough. Encourage them to be thinking all the time about what they might make. (If a child does not manage to complete an object in the allotted time, suggest that he might like to play with the dough some other time to make his creation for the group to see.) The game continues until everybody has had a turn. Finally, try to recall all the objects made during the course of the game.

Support
In the centre of the circle, place a collection of props such as lollipop sticks, buttons, string and matchsticks to stimulate the children's imaginations and enhance their creations.

Extension
Choose a theme for the game such as animals, people or transport to encourage the children to create more complex models.

HOME LINKS
Send home your favourite play dough recipe for parents to make up and use with their children.

The parrot parade

'Your mums and dads and grans and granddads are coming to assembly on Friday,' said Mrs Evans. 'We need to have something very special for them to see.' She sighed. 'But I don't know what. Has anybody got any good ideas?'

Jack, sitting at the back of all the rows of children, thought carefully.

'We could have a parade,' he said, excitedly.

Mrs Evans looked up. 'A parade,' she said. 'That sounds like a good idea.'

All the children clapped. Brilliant! A parade it would be.

'But a parade of what?' said Sophie impatiently.

'Parrots!' said Mrs Evans.

Everybody clapped again. A parade of parrots sounded excellent.

'But where are we going to get the parrots?' said Jack.

'That's easy,' said Mrs Evans, her eyes gleaming. 'We'll make them!'

Out came the scissors and the paper and the card and the pens and the pencils and the paints and the paintbrushes. Mrs Evans made a parrot, without any feathers, for each child. Then she cut out hundreds of feathers.

Mrs Evans said, 'Red group can paint red feathers. Yellow group can paint yellow feathers. Blue group can paint blue feathers. Green group can paint green feathers. Orange group can paint orange feathers. And purple group can paint purple feathers. Our parrots will be beautiful!'

Off went the children into their groups to do their painting. They painted and painted and painted. Then they all moved around to the next group. Red group moved on to paint yellow feathers. Blue group moved on to paint green feathers. Green group moved on to paint orange feathers. Orange group moved on to paint purple feathers. And purple group moved on to paint red feathers.

They painted and painted. Then they all moved on to the next group. Red group moved on to blue. Yellow group moved on to green. Green group moved to purple. Orange group moved to red. Purple group moved to yellow…

'STOP!' cried Mrs. Evans. 'This is much too hard! I can't remember where you're supposed to move to next! Everybody — just paint the feathers you want to paint — red or blue or yellow or green or orange or purple!' So they did. And when the feathers were all finished, they were stuck onto a cut-out parrot. The beaks were coloured in white and the beady eyes in black.

And then the children practised the parade. Wow! Jack was so proud that it was his idea. Everybody agreed that the Parrot Parade would probably be the best assembly ever.

And do you know what? It was.

© Irene Yates

Farmyard friends

Farmyard friends

Secret shopping

Alphabet bingo

q			n		b
t		d		f	
		h	s		c
v		i		l	

u		j		g	
		p	m		a
w		r		k	
y				o	e

How many does that make?

1 •	2 ••	3 •••
4 ••••	5 •••••	
••• 6 •••	••• 7 ••••	•••• 8 ••••
•••• 9 •••••	••••• 10 •••••	

Where is it?

Let's make a butterfly

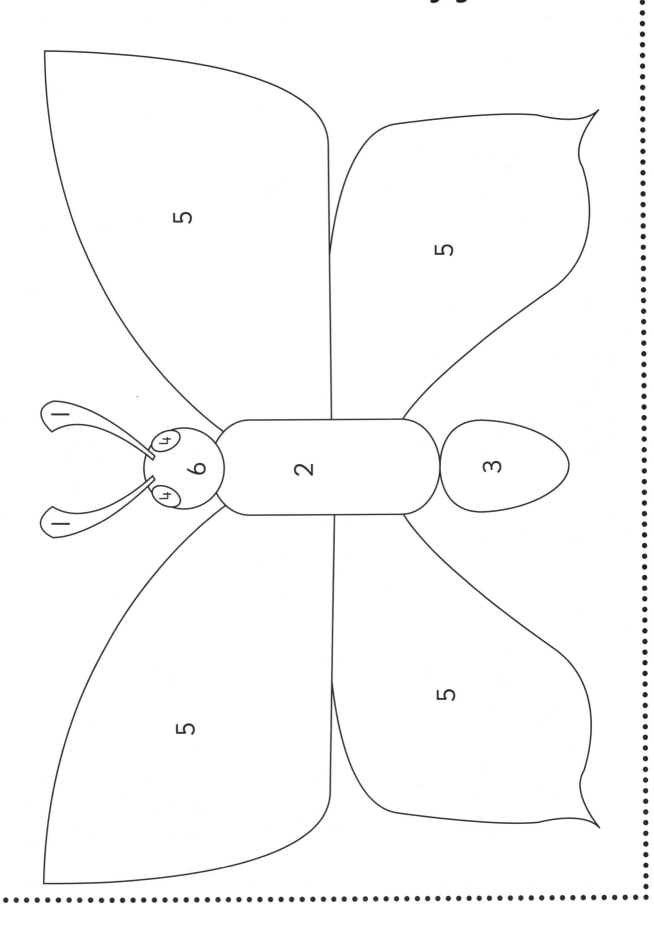

Let's make a butterfly

What shall I wear?

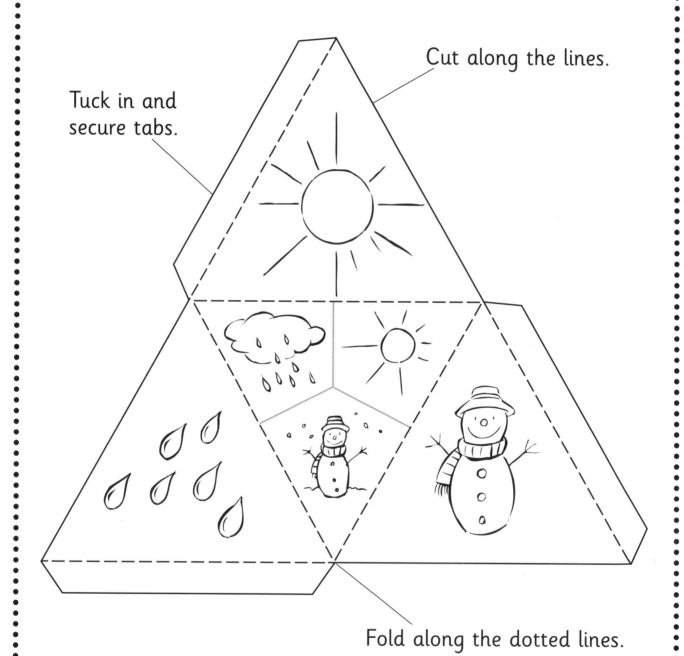

Tuck in and
secure tabs.

Cut along the lines.

Fold along the dotted lines.

What shall I wear?

Ceiling, floor, window, door

Cut out the words and stick them onto the correct body parts.

head	shoulder	knee	elbow
foot	arm	leg	hand

I sent a postcard to my friend

To

_____

From

_____

I sent a postcard to my friend

Tiles and more tiles

Fun with colours

Fun with colours